100 THINGS BROWNS FANS SHOULD KNOW & DO BEFORE THEY DIE

100 THINGS BROWNS FANS SHOULD KNOW & DO BEFORE THEY DIE

Zac Jackson

Library of Congress Cataloging-in-Publication Data available upon request

This book is available in quantity at special discounts for your group or organization. For further information, contact:

Triumph Books LLC
814 North Franklin Street
Chicago, Illinois 60610
(312) 337-0747
www.triumphbooks.com

Printed in U.S.A.
ISBN: 978-1-62937-730-8
Design by Patricia Frey

To Browns fans everywhere, who
have seen some, um, stuff.

To my dad, who allowed me to appreciate and consume all things football but for a long time had me believing you had to leave at some point during the third quarter.

Contents

1 All the Way Back, Almost

On January 5, 2003, the Cleveland Browns were back. Finally.

Technically, they'd been back in the NFL for a while. There were guys in orange helmets playing on Sundays at one o'clock, anyway. But it wasn't until their fourth season that the Browns finally started winning games. They snuck in the playoffs and drew the hated Pittsburgh Steelers as their opponent, a sign that the Cleveland Browns were truly back.

Thanks to old owner Art Modell's shady dealings, the Browns were gone for three years. The old team had become the Baltimore Ravens and won the Super Bowl in 2000. The new team wasn't quite the one Paul Brown and Jim Brown and Lou Groza had made a power, or the one that kept flirting with the Super Bowls in the 1980s, but the Browns were finding their stride.

For their first two years back in the league, they were an expansion team that showed little progress. The hiring of Butch Davis as coach ahead of the third year brought a jolt, and in 2002 the Browns were good enough to be a relevant NFL team. That 2002 team was far from exceptional, but quarterback Tim Couch was making progress and the Browns went 6–2 on the road to put themselves in playoff contention.

Al Lerner, the owner of the new team, had died during the 2002 season. That week, the Browns rallied from 15 points down to win. In December, the Browns won in Jacksonville on a 50-yard Hail Mary from Couch to Quincy Morgan with no time left. There was more than a little magic with that 2002 team, which found a way to win its season finale even after Couch suffered a broken leg. Kelly Holcomb came off the bench to give the Browns a chance, and rookie running back William Green sprinted for a touchdown. The defense followed with a goal line stand, and later in the day, the teams the Browns needed to win won. The teams they needed to lose did. And the Browns were back in the playoffs.

That Sunday in Pittsburgh, the pesky underdog Browns were leading the Steelers 24–7 in the third quarter.

The Browns had officially been reborn on September 7, 1998, the day the NFL awarded an expansion franchise to Lerner and declared that the new Browns could keep the name, the logo, the history, everything that had made the Browns one of the iconic NFL franchises and made their sudden departure so hard to fathom.

On September 12, 1999, the new Browns played their first game. They lost, 43–0, to the Steelers, but those things happen to expansion teams. And despite Lerner paying $530 million for the Browns, at the time the highest price tag in pro sports history, the Browns were an expansion team. The week after that 43–0 beating they started Couch, the No. 1 pick of the new era, and upward a long climb began.

So, finally, the Browns were back, and the Steelers were reeling and all the waiting and work to get Cleveland its team back seemed worth it.

But a journeyman named Tommy Maddox turned into Superman. Per orders of their head coach, the Browns were sitting back in a prevent defense and Maddox kept shredding them. The Browns needed just one defensive play but couldn't make it. Late in the game, a young Browns wide receiver named Dennis Northcutt was wide open on the sideline for what would have been a monster first down.

Northcutt dropped the pass.

Holcomb threw for 429 yards, but the Browns still lost. The Steelers scored 22 points in the fourth quarter—the final 15 of the game—and advanced, winning 36–33.

Sixteen years later, the new Browns were still trying to get back to the playoffs. Through multiple owners, multiple coaches, and 30 quarterbacks, they'd mostly lost. Three years after that game in Pittsburgh, Couch, Green, and Courtney Brown would all be out of the NFL. Davis won 16 games in his first two seasons with the Browns and eight in the next two.

The losses mounted. Change became the only constant. The Browns went 1–15 in 2016, and then did the nearly impossible by not winning a single game the year after that. From January 2003 to January 2019, the Browns beat the Steelers only four times.

For 50 or so minutes that day in Pittsburgh, though, the Browns were almost back. Almost two decades later, the climb was still on.

2 Miss after Miss (after Miss)

The story of the first 20 seasons of the new-era Browns essentially starts with the number 1 and ends with the number 30.

The Browns made the playoffs once from 1999 to 2018. Thirty is how many quarterbacks started games for the Browns from the time Ty Detmer kept the seat warm for Tim Couch for all of one game in 1999 until Baker Mayfield, the No. 1 pick in the 2018 draft, took over three games into the 2018 season. The Browns were so bad that they got the No. 1 pick in consecutive years. They got to that astounding number of 30 through bad drafting, bad luck, and bad play.

Starting with Couch, the first pick of the new franchise and the No. 1 overall pick in 1999, the Browns tried five times to find their quarterback in the first round. Brady Quinn was popular but far from exceptional. Brandon Weeden was a flier who never really got off the ground. Johnny Manziel was a complete disaster, on and off the field, starting in his first few weeks with the team.

Mid-round picks like Charlie Frye and Colt McCoy didn't work either. The Browns also tried the retread route. Kelly Holcomb was exceptional for one game and mediocre in most others. Derek Anderson was claimed on waivers and made the Pro Bowl in 2007, but Anderson never recaptured that magic in the years that followed. Jeff Garcia was an unlikely Pro Bowler in San Francisco. In his one season with the Browns, he was far from good.

Brian Hoyer was the third-stringer for his first four months with the Browns. He then won his first three starts before suffering a torn ACL. He came back the next year and played well for a stretch before getting replaced by Manziel. That season went up in flames. Hoyer left a few months later via free agency and Manziel was cut a year later. Josh McCown was good enough in one stretch to become the first Browns quarterback to throw for 300 yards in three straight games.

From 2003 to 2012, the Browns only had the same Opening Day starting quarterback once, Charlie Frye in 2006–07. Frye was traded two days after the 2007 opener, a game the Browns lost 34–7. After Weeden started consecutive openers in 2012–13, the Browns had a different starting quarterback in each of their next five openers.

The modern-day NFL is a quarterback-driven league. From 2008 to 2016, the Browns started at least three different quarterbacks in a season six times. If you wonder how the Browns had five different head coaches between 2008 and 2014, or how stretches like 4–44, 1–31, and the 0–16 season in 2017 happened, the answers lie within the ever-changing, ever-failing quarterback story.

The old Browns had Hall of Famer Otto Graham, then much later they had Brian Sipe and Bernie Kosar. The new Browns had Spergon Wynn and Cody Kessler. In 2017 the Browns drafted

DeShone Kizer in the second round. Kizer was an early entry with a big arm and much to learn. He had no business playing as a rookie, but the Browns started him anyway. By mid-October he was so overwhelmed that Hue Jackson gave Kizer a week off. Kizer wasn't benched, but rather had the opportunity to step back and watch the Texans embarrass another young quarterback, Kevin Hogan, and an overmatched Browns team. Kizer returned to play the next week, and he played the rest of the season.

The Browns went 0–16. They had been 1–15 the season before that, and 3–13 the season before that. That stretch of 4–44 over three seasons was the worst in NFL history. The Browns traded for Tyrod Taylor before the 2018 season, making him their bridge quarterback ahead of drafting Mayfield at No. 1 overall. Taylor got all the starter's snaps through training camp and the preseason, but when he got injured in a Week 3 game vs. the Jets, Mayfield entered and brought the Browns back from a two-score deficit.

Mayfield threw for 201 yards as the Browns won, 21–17. The Browns snapped a 19-game winless streak and won for the first time in 635 days. They went on to finish the season at 7–8–1 after Jackson and offensive coordinator Todd Haley were fired at mid-season. Mayfield set a new NFL record for most touchdown passes by a rookie with 27, and Freddie Kitchens was hired as head coach after calling the plays in the second half of the season.

The Browns went forward believing the interminable quarterback carousel would stop with Mayfield, at No. 30. Their next objective was changing the number of playoff appearances in the new era to a number higher than one.

3 No Ordinary Joe

Joe Thomas was never a suit-and-tie guy. So it was fitting that when the Browns drafted the future of Hall of Famer with the No. 3 pick in the 2007 Draft, Thomas wasn't on the stage in Radio City Music Hall to shake the hand of NFL commissioner Roger Goodell and stage a prolonged smile for dozens of cameras.

Thomas went fishing with his father on Lake Michigan. He had a fishing pole in one hand and his phone in the other when the call came from Browns general manager Phil Savage that afternoon. Savage told Thomas that he'd be picked by the Browns and would immediately become the team's starting left tackle. For an organization that both before and after struggled to make a first-round pick who even became a consistently good player, let alone a star, the Thomas pick was a hit. Thomas ended up playing 10,363 consecutive snaps over 11 seasons for the Browns before a torn triceps made him realize it was time to walk away. He went to the Pro Bowl in each of his first 10 seasons.

We don't know what fish Thomas and his father caught on April 28, 2007, but the Browns were in danger of not catching the right fish that day. Savage had an affinity for JaMarcus Russell, the physically gifted LSU quarterback who ended up just being big—and a big bust. Both Savage and Russell were natives of Mobile, Alabama, and Savage saw Russell as strong enough to throw the ball successfully through the elements in Cleveland—and in Pittsburgh, Cincinnati, and Baltimore, too.

The always unpredictable Raiders took Russell at No. 1, vaulting Thomas to the top of the Browns' board. Though the Browns had strongly considered five players—Russell, Thomas,

Joe Thomas blocks Terrell Suggs during a September 2016 game in Cleveland.
(Joe Robbins/Getty Images)

running back Adrian Peterson, wide receiver Calvin Johnson, and quarterback Brady Quinn—with their top selection, they had solid intel that the Detroit Lions would select Johnson at No. 2 and had long eyed Thomas as the pick if Russell was off the board. Quinn was an Ohio native who'd grown up a Browns fan. Discreetly, Savage had reached out to Quinn's representation just before the draft and informed them that Quinn wouldn't be the Browns' pick at No. 3, hoping to lessen the disappointment in case TV cameras focused on Quinn in the wake of the Browns making their selection.

Quinn ended up becoming the last player in the draft's green room, waiting until the 22nd pick before the Browns won a mad scramble and worked out a trade with the Cowboys to get back into the first round and select Quinn. Though the Browns spent nearly an hour making calls while trying to work out a deal to draft Quinn, Savage had come into that draft with a plan to do what he ended up doing, trade the team's 2008 first-round pick and whatever else it took to get back in the first round and bring another highly rated prospect into the fold.

He'd had some preliminary discussions with the Minnesota Vikings centering around Braylon Edwards, a top-five pick in 2005 and the first Browns' pick of the Savage era. Edwards went on to set a bunch of franchise records in 2007, but before that season his production had not matched his ego. As the draft unfolded, Savage called the Vikings, but they didn't call back. They had settled on taking Peterson at No. 7, and history proved that was the right pick.

Savage then began calling around in hopes of landing Cal running back Marshawn Lynch, but he found no takers before the Bills selected Lynch at No. 12. The Browns had a glaring need at cornerback at the time, too, and had graded Pitt's Darrelle Revis as a top-10 prospect. But the Jets told Savage they wouldn't trade out because they liked Revis, too, and after going to the Jets at No. 14 and going on to a hugely successful career, Revis will likely join Thomas in the Pro Football Hall of Fame. The attention of the room then turned to landing Quinn, whose long day got longer after the quarterback-needy Dolphins instead selected wide receiver Ted Ginn Jr. at No. 9.

The Bengals held pick No. 18 but had never traded with the Browns and weren't interested in doing so. The Titans and Giants, picking at Nos. 19 and 20, respectively, had zeroed in on their preferred targets and wouldn't lower their asking prices. Savage was worried that his old team, the Baltimore Ravens, would execute a trade to beat the Browns to Quinn. The Browns also received intel that the Kansas City Chiefs, who held pick No. 23, had been calling around about a trade up. Finally, after defensive backs had come off the board with four consecutive picks, Savage and Cowboys owner Jerry Jones worked out a deal to give the Browns pick No. 22 and end Quinn's long wait.

Ironically, Thomas would later say that part of the reason he'd skipped the draft was the 2005 experience of quarterback Aaron Rodgers, who'd endured a painfully long wait in the draft's green room while ESPN cameras caught his every wince and nervous tick. Thomas wanted to go fishing with his dad because that had long been their springtime Saturday routine, but he also didn't want to end up sweating for a national audience in case the draft didn't work out the way he'd believed it would.

"That left an impression on me for them to abuse a player like that, that's doing that for free," Thomas said. "I thought that was really tough."

Rodgers ended up doing quite well for himself. Things worked out in both the short and long-term for Thomas, too. Even though he didn't go to New York, Thomas didn't have to wait. Quinn did though. Thomas ended up blocking for 22 different starting quarterbacks over his career. Quinn was one of them, but not The One that Browns fans had long been waiting for.

4 The Greatest

This book focuses on the new Browns, but it couldn't be a Browns book if we didn't discuss No. 32.

The standard is pretty high at the running back position. Three Browns running backs are in the Hall of Fame, and more than 50 years after walking away from football, Jim Brown is still commonly referred to as "The Greatest."

Through 2019, Brown had the six most productive rushing seasons in Browns' history and seven of the top nine. Jamal Lewis is the only other Browns' running back to top 1,300 yards in a season.

A three-time NFL MVP, Brown had 12,312 rushing yards in his career. He led the NFL in rushing eight times and is the only running back in NFL history to average over 100 yards per game for his career. His NFL rushing record stood until Walter Payton broke it in 1984, and through 2019 he was the only player to have led the NFL in all-purpose yards five times.

Brown had a pair of 17-rushing-touchdown seasons, in 1958 and again in 1965. With the Browns, Leroy Kelly is next on that list with 16 touchdowns in 1968 and 15 two years earlier. Brown also had a 14-touchdown season in 1959 and had 13 rushing touchdowns in 1962 on his way to 106 for his career.

Brown was inducted into the Pro Football Hall of Fame in 1971. Bobby Mitchell, a running back who also played wide receiver because his four years coincided with Brown's, was

Jim Brown runs over the opposition. (Tony Tomsic/AP Photo)

inducted in 1983. Kelly was inducted in 1994 after making six Pro Bowls and twice leading the NFL in rushing. For perspective on just how dominant Brown was, Kelly had 74 career rushing touchdowns.

In 1966, Brown retired while on the set of *The Dirty Dozen* in London. Brown had already been pointing towards an acting career, and when owner Art Modell threatened to fine him for missing the start of training camp due to production delays, Brown chose to retire rather than continue to squabble with Modell.

He continued to pursue an acting career through the 1970s. He later did some TV work, and in 1988 he founded the Amer-I-Can program designed to help troubled youth, prisoners, and gang members in Cleveland and Los Angeles develop life skills to turn their lives around. Despite multiple charges of assault and domestic violence against women, Brown was hired by then-owner Randy Lerner as a special consultant to the Browns in 2008. Since then he's had an on-again, off-again relationship with the team, but he's served in a special advisor's role to Jimmy Haslam since 2013.

5 Phil Dawson

Who scored the first rushing touchdown of the Browns' new era?

The kicker did, of course. Phil Dawson scored a bunch of points for the Browns, and after arriving in 1999 with no promises he'd make it even a month, he didn't leave the organization until 2013. Dawson's run with the Browns spanned 14 seasons and saw him score 1,271 points, the second most in franchise history.

He'd only made two field goals for the 1999 expansion Browns when he scored that rushing touchdown, taking a pitch on a fake field goal from holder and friend Chris Gardocki and beating the stunned Bengals to the pylon on a four-yard touchdown run. The Browns lost that game, 18–17, but Dawson accounted for 11 points.

By the time Dawson left for the 49ers in 2013, he was a Pro Bowler who'd played for five different full-time head coaches and made 305 field goals. His 84 percent success rate on those kicks was the best among the 27 kickers in NFL history who at the time had made at least 300 field goals. Dawson had come to the Browns after going undrafted and getting cut loose by the Patriots, and during his first month with the team he made a startling discovery one day while leaving work. In the parking lot he encountered a van being driven by a team employee. In the back of the van were four or five kickers, all of whom had been flown in by the team's decision-makers for a workout.

Dawson almost met his replacement on his way out the door. But he kept his job, then and for years to come, with a series of clutch kicks and a consistency molded by his relentless work ethic. In 2010, Dawson surpassed Hall of Fame kicker Lou Groza for first place on the Browns' all-time field goal list with his 235th make.

After a decorated career at the University of Texas and a year on the Patriots' practice squad, Dawson landed with the Browns during the dial-up internet era. He stayed so long that when he left, he delivered a farewell message via Twitter.

"Hey, Cleveland. Thank you for a tremendous ride," Dawson wrote. "Your love, support, and encouragement have blessed me deeply. Playing for you has been one of the great joys of my life, and I wish you all the best."

He was all class, all the way. He made three of the most famous field goals in the Browns' new era, starting with a 39-yarder in the final seconds as the Browns won in Pittsburgh's Three Rivers Stadium in November 1999. The Steelers had won the first game that year—the Browns' first game back in the NFL—43–0, so the revenge was sweet.

His 51-yard field goal on the final play of regulation in 2007 in Baltimore was originally ruled no good, and the Ravens left the field believing they'd won that game. But after a lengthy discussion by the officiating crew, the officials correctly ruled that the kick had gone through the uprights before hitting the stanchion behind the crossbar and bouncing back into the field of play. The Browns went on to complete their only season sweep of the Ravens with another Dawson field goal in overtime.

Later that season, Dawson accounted for 75 percent of the Browns' points in an 8–0 December win over the Bills, an especially memorable game because it was played in blizzard-like conditions with winds approaching 40 MPH. After successfully guiding a 35-yarder through the elements and the uprights earlier in the game, Dawson was called upon again by coach Romeo Crennel to kick a 49-yard field goal into Cleveland Browns Stadium's west end. Dawson started the kick well to the right of the goalpost, and both the brave fans and the weather-tested kicker celebrated as the wind pushed that kick almost 15 yards back to the left and through the uprights.

"I don't know how it could have gotten much more difficult than it was," Dawson later said of that day. "Snow everywhere, and not only coming down but already on the ground. You couldn't see the field. You had no idea where you were. The wind was just ridiculous. It was cold, not quite as cold as some of the other ones we've had here. But when you mix all that together, it was a pretty brutal day.

"In warm-ups I missed one to the left. It stopped in mid-air, turned around and came back through the other way. It was one of those days. There were no rules that apply to that day."

That was an especially brutal day in a stadium that's long been hard on kickers, even those used to the conditions. The Browns' day-to-day operations are about 15 miles southwest of Downtown Cleveland in Berea, but Dawson made a point of practicing at the stadium at least once a week anytime the weather and swirling Lake Erie winds might be a factor. From Thursday through Sunday mornings during the season, he remained in near constant contact with the Browns' groundskeeping crew for the latest weather and field-condition updates. He worked like he was worried he'd see another van full of kicking prospects pull into the team's headquarters trying to take his job.

When Dawson was a free agent before the 2005 season, he went on a visit to the Buffalo Bills. After later signing a five-year

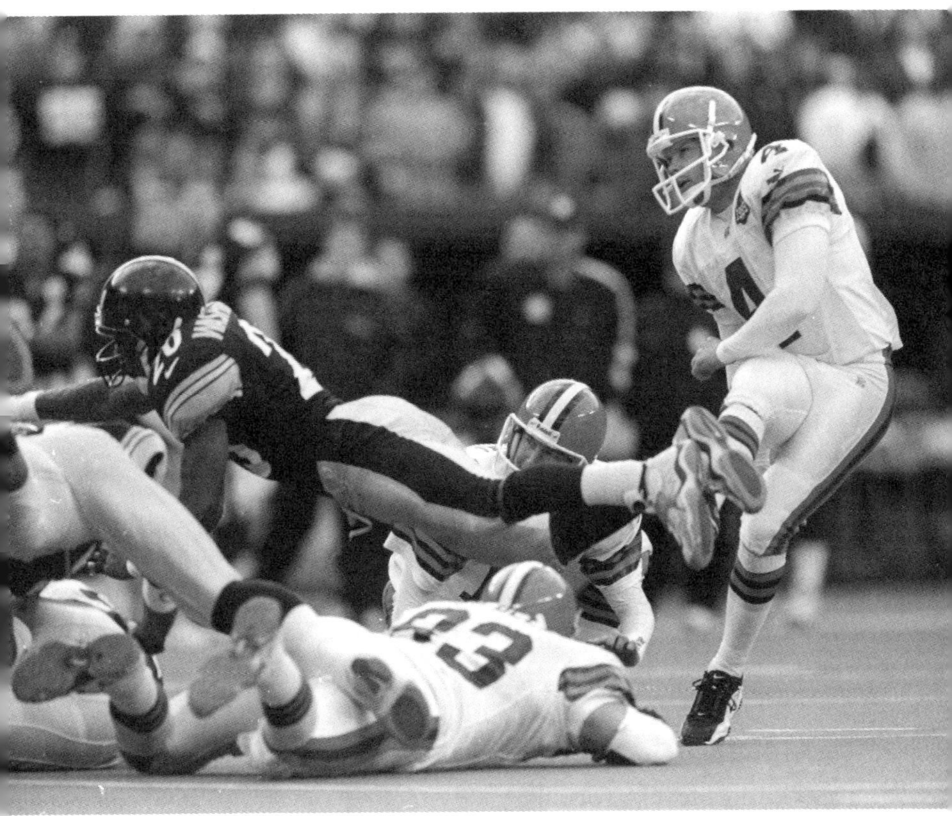

Phil Dawson kicks the game-winning field goal to beat the Steelers, 16–15, in November 1999. (Jamie Squire/Allsport/Getty Images)

extension to stay with the Browns, he likened that visit to feeling like he was cheating on his girlfriend. In a cut-throat business, he wanted to reward the Browns for their initial belief in him. He was at the top of his game when that new contract expired, and the Browns for the first time used the franchise tag to keep Dawson off of the open market. The team used the same tag the following year, and Dawson was named to the Pro Bowl in 2012 before leaving to sign with the 49ers before 2013. He went from replaceable player to franchise player.

Near the end of the 2012 season, he wrote inside the shoe closet next to his locker, "Phil was here, 1999–2012." That locker has since been removed as the locker room was redone, but it will be a long time before anyone replaces Dawson in the team's record books.

6 Mr. Reliable

There are really no stats to measure the performance of a left tackle, the possible exception being the number of times the quarterback he's protecting either takes or avoids a monster hit.

Joe Thomas protected a lot of quarterbacks. Dozens of them. So many that in a televised feature on Thomas' sustained greatness ahead of what would become his final NFL season, the interviewer asked Thomas to name them all. And Thomas couldn't do it.

"I spent a lot of time at it," Thomas said. "I don't think I named all of them. I was, like, really close but there were the middle ages of my life, like years five to seven of my career, that it was just really hard to remember who was the quarterback back then."

Thomas wasn't perfect, and there were times those quarterbacks got hit. But Thomas was darn good for a long time. He was reliable, consistent, never asked out as the Browns kept losing, and always kept performing. By the time he officially called it quits after 11 seasons, he'd played in 10 straight Pro Bowls and six times been named All-Pro.

It would have been 11 straight Pro Bowls if not for the torn triceps that snapped his consecutive play streak at 10,363, a number the Browns would later retire inside FirstEnergy Stadium as the first of many ways the team honored his contributions.

It wasn't just that injury that pushed Thomas to retire. It was an accumulation of wear and tear. He'd dealt with lingering knee issues. Each year, Thomas said, it was taking him longer and longer every week to get his body ready to take part in a practice or two, and even more difficult to make sure he was spry enough to play every Sunday. Over his final seasons he'd generally only practice once per week, wouldn't play in the preseason, and sometimes wouldn't practice at all.

If the Browns hadn't been so awful in 2016 and had been chosen for a Thursday night game in early 2017, the streak might have been in jeopardy.

A few days before that ESPN preseason feature on Thomas aired, Thomas talked of being "uncomfortable" in the spotlight and joked that the network's "ratings are going to plummet." He was never a self-promoter and always self-deprecating. When ESPN made an error with a graphic during a preseason game that mistakenly called Thomas "the first offensive lineman ever," his linemates got t-shirts to honor Thomas and his longevity.

Before DeShone Kizer and Kevin Hogan became the 19th and 20th quarterbacks for whom Thomas blocked, he ended up naming all 18 for the ESPN cameras. The Browns kept changing around him. The Browns kept failing. But Thomas kept working, kept performing, and he rarely disappointed.

When he went down on the field during that game against the Titans and his streak came to an end, one of the players to run over and show Thomas a sign of respect was Taylor Lewan of the Titans, who at the time was becoming one of the game's best young left tackles.

"It ripped my heart out to see Joe Thomas go down like that," Lewan said after the game. "That dude is what so many of us aspire to be. He's a true pro and a great guy, too."

7 Quite a Find

Joe Thomas, the best player of the first 20 years of the Browns' new era, played tackle at Wisconsin, a program known for producing NFL offensive lineman. Though he went undrafted after setting multiple Texas records, kicker Phil Dawson was surrounded by fellow future NFL players during his time in Austin.

One of the greatest return men in NFL history was a quarterback at Kent State.

Josh Cribbs had never returned kickoffs or punts before signing with the Browns in the hours following the completion of the 2005 Draft. He'd never played wide receiver or played on special teams at all. The Browns offered Cribbs the chance to make the team as a special teams player or possibly a practice squad developmental prospect. He took it, and by the time he took off on a 90-yard kickoff return touchdown in his fourth NFL game, he was on his way to becoming a star.

Through 2018, his eight career kickoff return touchdowns remained tied for the most in NFL history. He led the NFL with three kickoff return touchdowns in 2009, two years after most teams had stopped giving him a fair chance to beat them in the return game. For much of his career, Cribbs was nearly as good on kick coverage units as he was as a return specialist.

When his record-setting college career ended, Cribbs knew he probably wasn't going to get drafted. He'd been arrested on a minor marijuana charge and served a one-game suspension in college, and small-school prospects with baggage always face an uphill battle even when they aren't making a position change.

Josh Cribbs returns a kick for a touchdown against the Vikings on September 13, 2009. (Dilip Vishwanat/Getty Images)

His hometown team, the Redskins, had offered him the chance to stay at quarterback. But Cribbs knew his NFL future—if there was going to be one—would be at a different position. Or maybe a bunch of positions. He'd been recruited as a defensive back out of high school by some major college programs, but he always felt most comfortable with the ball in his hands. He'd never returned kicks or punts at any level until getting to the pros.

Kent State is only about an hour's drive from the Browns' day-to-day headquarters, and Cribbs' college numbers were good enough to draw attention from multiple NFL teams. But it was at a now-defunct January all-star game in Las Vegas that Cribbs made his first real impression on the Browns. Scout Kevin Kelly was there, specifically focused on the wide receivers, and he kept watching Cribbs over the three days of practice.

"The competitiveness, it just jumped out at you," Kelly said. "He didn't know how to run a route. His hands weren't in the perfect place to be ready for the pass. But he found a way to catch it. He battled the defender and shook him, even if it wasn't with perfect technique. I just kept watching him because I knew there was something there, and I hoped eventually we could get it out of him."

The Browns made Cribbs a priority free agent, ultimately giving him a $5,000 signing bonus to try to make the team as a backup wide receiver and special teams player. And though he still struggled with the finer points of the wide receiver position, it quickly became clear that Cribbs was a project worth taking on. As a returner, he never shied away from contact. He was patient as a runner from his days as a shotgun quarterback, and in the 2005 preseason he showed no hesitation in making tackles on kick coverage.

"There were times that I wondered if I was doing the right thing out there, and early on I always wondered if I was still going to be on the team the next day," Cribbs would later say. "But I never feared anything on the field. I never feared getting cut. I just knew I had to leave it all out there."

The Browns had drafted Braylon Edwards at No. 3 overall in 2005 with the intent of making him their No. 1 receiver, which Edwards eventually became. But further down the depth chart, Cribbs made himself so valuable that the Browns moved on from Lance Moore, another priority free agent at the position. Moore would eventually catch on with the Saints, where he had a good enough career to be inducted into the team's hall of fame.

Similar recognition for Cribbs will eventually come from the Browns, too. Through various regimes and roles, Cribbs continued to give up his body but never give up on a play. His zigging, zagging, and spinning 2007 kickoff return touchdown in Pittsburgh is the kind of play that makes NFL Films highlight reels for decades. He played for the Browns through 2012, then, after signing a contract with the Raiders but never playing for them, had brief stays with the Colts and Jets. By then, Cribbs had little left in his body. In 124 games with the Browns, he'd used it all up.

8 Less than Mangenius

Eric Mangini's first NFL job was with the Browns. He was a ball boy. He worked in the equipment room. Later, he became a public relations assistant before eventually landing the lowest-level job as an offensive assistant on Bill Belichick's staff in 1995, the final year of the old franchise.

After one season working with the Ravens, Mangini reunited with Belichick with the Jets, then followed him to the Patriots in 2000 and became a position coach for the first time. After four years coaching defensive backs, Mangini became Belichick's defensive coordinator. Before they became rivals—and enemies once Mangini turned Belichick in for videotaping a Rams practice leading up to the Super Bowl—theirs was a teacher and protégé relationship.

Mangini's best win as head coach of the Browns was a 34–14 domination of Belichick and the Patriots on November 7, 2010. The Browns came into that game at 2–5, but rolled up a season-high 404 yards of offense, 230 on the ground.

Picking Mangini's best win with the Browns isn't that difficult. His Browns teams went 5–11 in both of his seasons on the job, 2009 and 2010. He'd been the head coach of the Jets for three seasons before getting fired at the end of the 2008 season, and then-Browns owner Randy Lerner hired him shortly thereafter.

The 2009 Browns were awful—and a mess off the field, too. They started 1–11 before winning four straight. George Kokinis, hired as general manager even though Mangini was calling all the shots, was fired at midseason. Mangini's director of operations, Erin O'Brien, was also fired during the season. Mangini traded away Kellen Winslow Jr. and Braylon Edwards. Mangini wanted older players who were smart and versatile enough to play multiple positions, often at the expense of those players being good enough to impact games. The last round of the Derek Anderson vs. Brady Quinn quarterback competition resulted in no winner, and both players were jettisoned before the next season.

Mangini tried too hard to be Belichick. Cutting talented players with big egos or other baggage only works when other talented players are on hand. Mangini grabbed too much power, too soon, and the Browns were a mess as a result. In the aftermath of Kokinis' strange exit and Mangini's roster overhaul, Lerner began a search for what he called "a strong, credible football leader" that led to the hiring of Mike Holmgren before the end of the 2009 season. Lerner had tried to hire Bill Cowher as head coach and

Scott Pioli as head of the football operations department before hiring Mangini, who was just 38 in 2009. But Lerner was always a bit infatuated with Mangini, and Lerner allowed the young coach to have too much power.

When that 2009 season ended, Holmgren and Mangini met over multiple days about the head coach's future with the team. Tom Heckert was hired as general manager, and ultimately Holmgren decided that Mangini and his staff would stay and that Heckert would take over the personnel decisions, though Holmgren still sat atop the organizational chart. It was an awkward setup that seemed doomed from the start. And it was.

The Browns were much better in Mangini's second season because they had better players, but also because the players had a much better grasp of Mangini's schemes and expectations. The emergence of running back Peyton Hillis certainly helped, and a power run game kept the defense off the field and sometimes allowed the defense to play with the lead. Hillis went from fullback and part-time player to rushing for 1,177 yards and making the cover of the popular Madden video game the next season.

But despite upsetting the Patriots and the Saints, the 2010 Browns didn't have enough offense to make a push for the playoffs. After some shaky game management cost them in an overtime loss to Mangini's old team, the Jets, the Browns turned the ball over six times in a loss in Jacksonville. They lost their last four games of that season, basically sealing Mangini's fate.

In retrospect, Holmgren never should have retained Mangini. They were too different, and clearly Holmgren had been given permission to find his own coaches. Holmgren said publicly that because he still saw himself as a coach, he didn't think it was fair for Mangini to only get one season with the Browns. But with no strong quarterback and Holmgren in power, Mangini never really had a chance.

In his five seasons as a head coach, Mangini's teams went 33–47. After leaving the Browns he worked three seasons as an assistant with the 49ers, the last as defensive coordinator under head coach Jim Tomsula in 2015. Mangini was doing some occasional TV work in the years that followed, but as of 2019 was not back in coaching.

9 Bad Luck, Bad Lines Hampered Couch

Linebacker Ryan Taylor played all of four games in a Browns uniform, so he shouldn't be a significant part of team history. But there's no doubt that a lot changed during a run-of-the-mill practice just short of the midway point of the 2000 season.

Tim Couch was throwing a pass in that practice when his right hand hit Taylor's arm. It was an awkward collision, and Couch immediately knew he'd suffered a significant injury. It ended up being a fractured thumb that required surgery and ended Couch's season.

It would be the first of three significant injuries Couch would suffer. The No. 1 pick in the 1999 NFL Draft ended up being done with football after the 2003 season due to chronic elbow issues. After playing his best football in 2002 in leading the Browns to the brink of the playoffs, Couch suffered a broken leg in the regular season finale and Kelly Holcomb started the only playoff game in the first 20 years of the team's new era.

The first pick of the expansion-era Browns unintentionally became a symbol for the new franchise's two decades of struggle and change: so much bad luck, so much draft-related disappointment, not enough good play from the game's most important position.

When Couch was lost for the 2000 season, that season was sunk. It quickly became clear that Chris Palmer, the first coach of the new era, would soon be replaced. No one expected the Browns to go from expansion team to immediate contender, but with few wins coming, team president Carmen Policy wanted make a splash with a new coaching hire. Couch stayed healthy in 2001 under new coach Butch Davis but was inconsistent and prone to making bad decisions at the wrong time. In 2002, he missed time in the preseason due to recurring elbow issues and suffered an October concussion, but he rebounded to play the most confident and most efficient football of his pro career.

But the broken leg led to Holcomb throwing for 429 yards in that playoff game, and that led to some inside the building thinking that Holcomb could be the answer for the Browns going forward. Then-offensive coordinator Bruce Arians always insisted that Couch was still young, still learning, and would have had a long career if not for the arm and elbow issues. Couch battled elbow tendinitis throughout his career and believes that led to shoulder issues. He ultimately had two shoulder surgeries that ended any thoughts he had of making a football comeback.

Couch had some magical moments, most notably the Hail Mary in New Orleans for the new franchise's first win in 1999 and another in 2002 in Jacksonville that kept that playoff push alive. He led a late touchdown drive in Baltimore in the penultimate game of the 2002 season to rescue an offense that had struggled for most of the last three quarters. The Browns finished that season 6–2 on the road, which doesn't happen without a little bit of luck and a lot of steady quarterback play.

The Browns' original plan had been to let Couch learn from veteran Ty Detmer in 1999 and slowly get comfortable with the

NFL game. He'd played in a wide-open, air raid-type offense at the University of Kentucky that didn't use a playbook. He'd obviously never dealt with the pressure of being the No. 1 pick and had rarely faced any kind of losing or personal struggle when it came to sports.

But the wait for Couch and the new Browns lasted all of one game. He ended up making 14 starts as a rookie and seven before the thumb injury in 2000. At that point, he'd thrown 22 touchdown passes and 22 interceptions, but he was sacked 56 times as a rookie. In 2001, he was sacked 51 times.

He endured 166 sacks in 62 career games.

"I think when a young guy gets thrown in a bad situation, it can kill his confidence," Couch said. "There were times I thought we were making good progress. There were times I thought I was really getting better, really getting the chance to put good games together and get comfortable with everything. But the injuries kept popping up, and I was getting hit a lot, and it takes a toll. I did lose confidence, and I just rarely got the chance to get it back."

After the Browns decided to move on from Couch and go with Jeff Garcia before the 2004 season, Couch signed a one-year deal with the Green Bay Packers. But the same arm and elbow issues limited his availability and his effectiveness, and the Packers cut Couch before the regular season began.

Couch had business interests back in Kentucky and dabbled in broadcasting after his playing career. In 2018, he was hired by the Browns as the color analyst for their preseason games. He'd previously made only a handful of trips back to Cleveland, where he ended up playing in 62 career games, throwing 64 touchdown passes, and 67 interceptions.

10 Ray Farmer's Many Whiffs

With Jimmy Haslam having taken ownership and placing Joe Banner in charge of the football operations, Banner had always planned to hire Mike Lombardi as general manager of the Browns following the 2012 season.

But the Browns also interviewed Ray Farmer. A former NFL linebacker, Farmer had gotten into scouting with the Falcons in the early 2000s and then had worked for the Chiefs, progressing to director of player personnel and becoming a candidate for external promotion.

Farmer was in a Cleveland-area hotel room when Banner and Haslam took off to Charlotte to complete the hiring of head coach Rob Chudzinski, awaiting the final word on the GM job that Lombardi would end up getting.

But then, a few months later, the Browns added Farmer as assistant general manager.

The next year, Banner and Lombardi were fired after just one season and Farmer was promoted in early 2014. At the time, it was hard to imagine anyone being less popular or less qualified for the job than Lombardi was. But Farmer was just getting started.

The Browns at the time were loaded with draft picks but also littered with holes. Partly because Banner and Lombardi were running the show and partly because the new Haslam ownership had fired Chudzinski after just one season, the Browns had several head-coaching candidates tell the team they weren't interested. But Haslam let Banner hire Mike Pettine before making the change, making for another awkwardly arranged marriage atop the football department.

During the lead-up to the 2014 Draft, Pettine never met Justin Gilbert, a cornerback prospect and draft early entry out of Oklahoma State. But after trading down five spots on draft night and then up one spot, Farmer selected Gilbert at No. 8. And that whole awkward at the top thing got even more awkward when a couple hours later, the Browns traded up again and selected quarterback Johnny Manziel at No. 22.

The Banner-led administration had long recommended avoiding the Manziel circus, long before most even knew how much of a circus it would actually become. Banner is on record in multiple formats saying that when he was fired by the Browns, Manziel was not even on the team's draft board.

But Haslam wanted Farmer to draft Manziel, and when the Eagles were willing to make the trade that night, Farmer and the Browns drafted Manziel. The attention Manziel drew kept Gilbert in the background, but Gilbert had maturity issues. He was disciplined multiple times for things like oversleeping and being late to meetings. On one road trip in his rookie season, he told coaches he wasn't sure he was feeling up to playing the next day. So the Browns just didn't play him.

At Gilbert's Oklahoma State pro day, a coach from another AFC team approached Gilbert after the formal workout. The coach explained that his team was in the market both for a cornerback and a boost in the return game, and that's why he'd flown to Oklahoma to get a closer look at Gilbert. The coach asked Gilbert if he'd catch some punts from the JUGS machine so the coach could get an evaluation on his technique.

Gilbert declined. That team removed Gilbert from its draft board. Later, multiple reports said other teams had major concerns about Gilbert's focus and his passion for football. The Browns took him anyway.

Later in that same draft the Browns traded up to take running back Terrance West. That trade was made so that the Browns could get in front of West's hometown team, the Ravens. But the Ravens weren't taking West, in part because they worried about his maturity and didn't want him around potential bad influences in Baltimore. West went on to play for both the Browns and the Ravens, but he didn't last long in the NFL.

In 2015, Farmer again had two first-round draft picks. He started at No. 12 by taking defensive tackle Danny Shelton, who had three average seasons with the Browns. He then took offensive lineman Cameron Erving at No. 19 despite Erving not having a spot on the offensive line—and not being good enough to earn one. Erving was traded before his third season to the Chiefs, where he became a starter.

Like Manziel and Gilbert, Farmer never got to a third season. Farmer and Pettine were fired not long after the Browns finished the 2015 season at 3–13. Before the 2016 season, the Sashi Brown–led Browns traded Gilbert to the Steelers for a late-round draft pick. He played one season in Pittsburgh as a backup and part-time kick returner. The Steelers cut Gilbert not long after that season, and he never played in the NFL again. In the New Browns' Bust Hall of Fame, his bust is one of the most prevalent—yet still overshadowed by Manziel's.

11 "Both of Those Days Were Phenomenal"

Having grown up two hours west of Cleveland in Toledo, Rob Chudzinski lived a dream in becoming head coach of the Cleveland Browns.

That it lasted just one season isn't the most unique part of the Chudzinski-Browns story. The new-era Browns have cycled through coaches, but Chudzinski is the only full-time coach to have been fired after one season.

The more staggering detail is this: Chudzinski was actually paid to leave the Browns three times. It's not exactly the American dream, but it's a very new-Browns story.

His first stint with the Browns came in 2004, as tight ends coach under then-coach Butch Davis. Chudzinski had played at the University of Miami (Fla.) and then coached there, progressing from graduate assistant to position coach to offensive coordinator from 2001 to '03. When Davis resigned under pressure late in the 2004 season, his staff was replaced a month or so later and Chudzinski became the tight ends coach with the San Diego Chargers.

But the Browns called again. Maurice Carthon had flopped as offensive coordinator and was fired during the 2006 season. On the hot seat himself, then-coach Romeo Crennel called on Chudzinski to be Carthon's replacement and ignite an offense that, after a messy quarterback competition and nightmarish start to the 2007 season, went on to set franchise passing records. Derek Anderson, Joe Thomas, Kellen Winslow Jr., and Braylon Edwards went to the Pro Bowl after the 2007 season, and Chudzisnki, Crennel, and other key members of the coaching staff got raises and extensions.

Everything went belly-up in 2008, and the entire staff was fired. Chudzinski went back to the Chargers, where he served as tight ends coach and assistant head coach. From there he was hired as offensive coordinator of the Panthers, and his work with a young Cam Newton drew notice from several teams. In early 2013, the Browns hired him as head coach, calling on a familiar name and a native son to call the shots for the team not long after the Haslam family had taken ownership and Joe Banner became CEO.

The 2013 Browns went 4–12, losing their last seven games. The decision to fire Chudzinski was made before the season finale in Pittsburgh, about 50 weeks into the four-year contract he signed. The Browns still owed Chudzinski about $10.5 million. It's generally easy to find NFL head coach contract details, but those of executives and assistant coaches aren't readily accessible. So while it's impossible to say exactly how much the Browns paid Chudzinski to leave the organization three times, it was a substantial amount.

When Thomas retired in early 2018, he paid homage to his first offensive coordinator and his short-time former coach in his sometimes-emotional-but-mostly-hilarious farewell press conference.

"Of course, another moment I'll never forget is the Rob Chudzinski era," Thomas said. "Both of those days were phenomenal."

Chudzinski is the only full-time coach in new or old Browns history, dating to 1946, to make it only one season.

12 Big Numbers on Both Sides

Jamal Lewis battered the Browns. Later, he played a key role on one of the best offenses in franchise history.

Lewis played his entire nine-year career in the AFC North Division, six seasons for the Ravens and three for the Browns. He was the 2003 AP NFL Offensive Player of the Year after running for 2,066 yards, and he crushed the Browns along the way. His 295-yard game in Baltimore in September 2003 was an NFL single-game record at the time, then, later that season, he ran for 205 yards against the Browns in Cleveland.

His season total against the Browns was 52 carries for 500 yards and four touchdowns. Those are video game numbers.

After three more years as the Ravens' workhorse back, Lewis hit free agency in 2007. Phil Savage, the Browns' GM at the time, had been a high-ranking member of the Ravens' personnel department when the Ravens drafted Lewis. Savage knew Lewis well, and he knew that Lewis' physical running style would play well in the AFC North. The Ravens had cut Lewis with thoughts of bringing him back at a lesser salary, but when talks between the sides failed to progress the Browns got Lewis on a one-year deal for $3.5 million.

Lawrence Vickers, the Browns' fullback at the time, was playing at the highest level of his career in leading the way for Lewis. The Browns had spent big in free agency to acquire guard Eric Steinbach from the Bengals, and it's now clear that the drafting of Joe Thomas at No. 3 overall in 2007 was a home run. The biggest plays in 2007 came via the vertical passing game, but Lewis chewed up tough yards and kept defenses honest. He got at least 20 carries for the 2007 Browns nine times and carried the ball at least 21 times in six of the last seven games.

Savage's recruitment of Lewis—and the big 2007 season Lewis put together—offered a lesson in modern-day free agency. Savage knew Lewis well, and he would often say "a hungry Jamal is a good Jamal." The Browns bet on Lewis being eager and healthy enough to make the Ravens regret letting him walk, and in 2007 he did.

Lewis ran for 1,304 yards and nine touchdowns for the Browns in 2007. He ran for 92 yards and a touchdown in Baltimore in November 2007 as the Browns scored a wild 33–30 overtime win.

Lewis was listed at 240 pounds. He was compact, powerful, and rarely shied away from contact. The Ravens had cut him believing he had lost a step, and he was clearly limited in 2005–06 by bone spur issues. But he had surgery to correct them, and though he wasn't as explosive in the back half of his career as he'd been in his first four seasons, Lewis still was an effective runner and made life difficult on would-be tacklers.

In late 2008, Lewis became the 24th player in NFL history to go over 10,000 career rushing yards. He also went over 1,000 for that season, an impressive feat given the offensive struggles the Browns had that year.

It's not that much of anything worked for the 2009 Browns, who started 1–11. But Lewis was clearly slowing down and was never comfortable with his role under the new coaching staff and offensive coordinator Brian Daboll. Lewis was placed on injured reserve late in the 2009 season due to a concussion and never played again.

Through 2019, he remained the Ravens' all-time leader in rushing yards (7,801) and touchdowns (45). For his career, he had 10,607 yards and 58 rushing touchdowns.

13 Braylon Edwards

The first pick of the Phil Savage–Romeo Crennel era exuded confidence. He entered the league with major endorsement deals and angled for more. When the Browns played their first *Monday Night Football* game in five years, Braylon Edwards ran out of the tunnel and delivered both a cartwheel and a back flip.

He caught five passes for 154 yards and a touchdown that night against the Giants, the defending Super Bowl champions. Edwards welcomed the spotlight, and for a while the Browns thought they had a dominant wide receiver. But Edwards went from setting a franchise record with 16 touchdown catches in 2007 to having just three the rest of his Browns' career. He was traded to the Jets in 2009, getting the kind of big-city attention he craved. But he never reached superstardom, or even close. His production never came near matching what it was in 2007, and his rise ended as quickly as it started.

Edwards was always kind of the belle of his own ball. He was confident, smart, and calculating. He dressed well. He knew someone was always watching, and seemed to hope lots of people were watching. He thrived on that.

He'd arrived as the No. 3 pick in the 2005 Draft after Savage decided the Browns needed a game-breaking receiver. Edwards had an intriguing combination of size and speed, as well as a knack for making contested catches. But he missed two games during his rookie season while dealing with a staph infection in his arm, then his rookie season ended prematurely after he suffered a torn ACL late in that season. He was able to play the full season in his second year, but the Browns were desperate for better quarterback play and for a fully healthy Edwards to take the next step.

In 2007, Derek Anderson was flinging the ball down the field with confidence. Edwards, Kellen Winslow Jr., and Joe Jurevicius were using their size and athleticism to go up and get even the passes there weren't thrown well, and the Browns developed one of the league's most dangerous passing offenses. Edwards caught three touchdown passes in a wild win over the Dolphins and had three more multiple-touchdown games en route to 1,289 receiving yards and his only Pro Bowl appearance.

The drops started to pop up the next season. The Browns offense fell off—and fast. Edwards had just three touchdown catches in 2008, and his body language didn't indicate happiness and more back flips were just around the corner.

As Savage would later say: "In 2007, Braylon caught 16 touchdown passes and we all got contract extensions. In 2008, Braylon had 16 drops and we all got fired."

When Edwards' play slipped, he sparred with fans and said he'd never win over Browns fans because of his Michigan roots. After Crennel had asked him not to charter a helicopter and fly to

Braylon Edwards makes a one-handed touchdown catch over Darrelle Revis on December 9, 2007, in East Rutherford, New Jersey, in a game where the Browns beat the Jets, 24–18. (Al Pereira/Getty Images)

Columbus for the 2006 Ohio State–Michigan game the day before the Browns played at home, Edwards did anyway, and he was late getting back to team responsibilities. He was fined and called to the principal's office, not for the first or last time.

When Rob Chudzinski was the Browns' offensive coordinator, he would often have colorful—and direct—words for Edwards about the receiver's habit of being fashionably late to the practice field. Edwards was a diva when he was dominating and a diva when he wasn't. After Savage and Crennel were fired, that act didn't play well with new coach Eric Mangini. Edwards was traded to the Jets in October 2009 for Chansi Stuckey, Jason Trusnik, and two mid-round draft choices.

Edwards caught four touchdown passes in his first season with the Jets and seven in 2010, when he averaged a career-best 17.1 yards per reception. But Edwards had been inconsistent on the field and often in trouble off of it, dealing with DUI charges in New York and multiple assault allegations. When the lockout ended in 2011 he signed a one-year deal with the 49ers for $3.5 million.

Edwards bounced around the league in his last two years. He played in nine games for the 49ers in 2011, then returned to the Jets briefly in 2012. After making one start in 10 games and catching one touchdown pass for the Seahawks in 2012, he never played again.

14 Missing on Manziel

The selection of Johnny Manziel in the 2014 Draft excited what had become a beaten-down fanbase. It put the Browns back in the national conversation. Over the ensuing 20 months, it just turned out to be the wrong kind of conversation.

Manziel was a celebrity quarterback. The first problem with Manziel as an NFL player—and there were many—was that he was much more interested in being a celebrity. He arrived as Johnny Football and the first freshman ever to win the Heisman Trophy. He left in disgrace, to put it nicely, and had done little to help the team.

On and off the field, Manziel was a disaster. He repeatedly embarrassed the Browns over two years, and during that time he went 2–6 as a starter. He went to an undisclosed rehab center in his first offseason as a pro. That would be his last NFL offseason, as the Browns, tired of his partying and disappointed in an assault charge involving an ex-girlfriend, were more than ready to cut him by 2016.

Both of his seasons ended with Manziel having been placed on the injured reserve list. He had one 300-yard passing game—372 at Pittsburgh in 2015, a game the Browns lost by 21—and never started more than three consecutive games. He got Mike Pettine fired after two years as head coach. He chased Kyle Shanahan away after one year as offensive coordinator. Ray Farmer never had a chance as general manager, but Farmer giving in to owner Jimmy Haslam's push to draft Manziel ensured that Farmer never had a chance.

Farmer had been suspended for the first four games of 2015 as punishment for violating NFL rules by texting to the Browns' sideline during games. He was essentially asking for the Browns to put Manziel in the game in place of Brian Hoyer. A story passed along by longtime Browns' play-by-play man Jim Donovan sums up both that situation and the Manziel saga. Once the 2014 Browns fell out of playoff contention and eventually made the switch, the Bengals feasted on Manziel in his first game. They mocked his signature money sign, too. At one point, Manziel came back to the sideline, sat next to Hoyer, and essentially said, "You didn't tell me this shit was this hard."

Manziel got hurt later that month, and the Browns had to play third-stringer Connor Shaw in their season finale at Baltimore. The day before that game, Manziel didn't show up for meetings and walkthrough. The Browns had to send team security officials to his apartment to wake him up. The next day, Pettine made Manziel and fellow 2014 first-round pick Justin Gilbert, who was also being disciplined for missing mandatory activities, watch that game from the locker room. Pettine treated Manziel and Gilbert more like eighth-graders than professional football players. They really left Pettine no other choice.

Hoyer was gone the next season, but Manziel still couldn't beat out Josh McCown in the preseason. McCown got hurt in the season opener, and Manziel threw two touchdown passes as the Browns won in Week 2 over the Titans. But McCown came back the following week, played well for a few weeks and Manziel only played in emergency duty until McCown's play slipped.

In November 2015, the Browns issued a press release of sorts, a well-crafted announcement by the team website's staff writer that said Manziel would be the starting quarterback when the team returned from its bye week. But when Manziel went back to Texas for the bye week and more pictures of Manziel drinking and partying surfaced on social media, the Browns rescinded their announcement and demoted Manziel to No. 3, behind McCown and Austin Davis.

"Everyone in this organization wants what's best for Johnny, just like we do for every player in the locker room," Pettine said. "I'm especially disappointed in his actions and behavior because he has been working very hard. The improvements he's made from last year have been tremendous, but he still has to consistently demonstrate that he has gained a good understanding of what it takes to be successful at the quarterback position on this level."

Manziel had promised the team he wouldn't bring any attention or further embarrassment over the bye week, but he loved rapping on Instagram. Brian Sipe had to live with Red Right 88. Bernie Kosar had to live with those losses to the Broncos. Manziel used his Money Phone to dial a quick trip out of the NFL.

One of the problems with Manziel is that everything you heard—every whisper, every rumor, every outrageous story—was at least somewhat believable. That's been a theme with the new-era Browns in general as they've stacked outrageously bad decisions and compiled bad results.

Manziel was placed on injured reserve at the end of the 2015 season. On the final weekend of the season, Manziel went to Las Vegas to party. He posted a picture on social media to make it appear that he was at home. It was later revealed that he wore a disguise in Las Vegas. He missed the game the next day, subjecting himself to a substantial fine from the team. But the Browns were long done with Manziel and his antics. He was back for the following day's season-end checkout meetings, and that would be his last time in the building. The Browns swallowed a salary-cap hit to cut him before the 2016 league year.

Manziel maintained a low profile for a while, vowing that he'd gotten sober and learned from his many incidents, specifically the assault charge. He played for two Canadian Football League teams in 2018. In early 2019, the CFL released a statement announcing not only that Manziel had been released by the Montreal Alouettes, but that CFL teams had been barred from signing him again. Shortly after, he signed with the new Alliance of American Football, a league that folded just a few weeks after Manziel signed.

15 Back to the Playoffs

Butch Davis had a presence. He had a deep voice, a bit of a Southern drawl, and he followed through on his initial promise to make the Browns a competitive team.

Davis had Super Bowl rings from his time as an assistant with the Cowboys. He had a high profile after resurrecting the University of Miami program. Two years in, Carmen Policy thought the Browns needed some sizzle, and Davis brought that when he was hired as head coach in early 2001.

But the story of the four years Davis was on the sideline ended up being a microcosm of the new franchise's first two decades. Davis got too much power, too soon, and the Browns never built on the momentum created in his first two seasons. The only difference between Davis and the coaches/regimes that followed him is that he actually won a little. The 2001 Browns went 7–9. The 2002 Browns went 9–7, and through 20 seasons that remained the only playoff appearance of the new era.

That Davis took over the defensive play-calling in that playoff game and the Browns blew a big lead sums up his stay in Cleveland. The Browns were never the same the next season, damaged by salary-cap issues, poor drafting and a yo-yo at quarterback between Tim Couch and Kelly Holcomb. Davis had pushed out Dwight Clark, the first head of the new Browns' personnel department. It was Davis who drove draft decisions that resulted in the Browns taking Gerard Warren and Winslow. His right-hand man in the front office was Pete Garcia, a man with little prior NFL experience who had helped Davis rebuild the University of Miami program.

The last-gasp play for Davis came in 2004 when the Browns signed Jeff Garcia to play quarterback. But Jeff Garcia was never better than just okay, prized rookie tight end Kellen Winslow Jr. got injured in the second game, and the Browns flopped. On Thanksgiving weekend, Holcomb threw for 413 yards, but the Browns lost for a fifth straight time in Cincinnati, 58–48. The defense had been okay but the offense had struggled prior to that shootout in Cincinnati that resulted in the second-highest scoring game in NFL history at the time.

Two days later, Davis was out and Terry Robiskie was named interim coach.

Davis liked to stretch the truth. He struggled to admit that not all decisions went in his favor, or that sometimes it just wasn't his team's day. When Jamal Lewis ran for a record 295 yards against the Browns in 2003, Davis told reporters the next day that the run defense was actually pretty solid—except for those three or four times Lewis just took off into the clear daylight. When Holcomb suffered a broken leg the next week, Davis said Holcomb had only "a teeny-tiny" fracture and might be able to play the following week.

All the way to the ugly end in 2004, he blamed the team's salary-cap situation on others and blamed some members of the local media for turning the fan base and new owner Randy Lerner against him. A former defensive line coach, Davis had built a strong defensive front in his first two years, but the Browns then lost Earl Holmes, Dwayne Rudd, and Jamir Miller, while Warren and Courtney Brown never played up to their draft position.

Davis officially resigned but somehow got his money from the Browns. He later resurfaced as head coach at the University of North Carolina but was fired in 2011 after four seasons amid an academic fraud scandal. Davis and Pete Garcia would later be reunited in South Florida when Davis was hired as head football coach at Florida International University by Garcia, the school's athletic director.

16 Earl Little's Big Claim

Earl Little was an average to above-average safety who thought he was an all-world safety. He was a good player and a great talker, on and off the field.

In the NFL, a little confidence never hurt. Little had, well, more than a little.

Little played in parts of eight NFL seasons, making 52 career starts and racking up 18 career interceptions. At one point he took the Browns to task publicly for not helping him get in the Pro Bowl. He had six interceptions in 2003 and had a case, but on a losing team he was going to have to do more than he did to finish the season in Hawaii.

Speaking of talking your way into greatness, Little also took at least some of the credit for the new franchise's first win over the Steelers. Trailing 15–13 at Three Rivers Stadium in Week 10 of the 1999 season, the Browns had driven inside the Steelers' 25-yard line but had no timeouts left. Eventually, the field goal team came running onto the field. Phil Dawson, the kicker, was last.

With maybe two or three seconds left, holder Chris Gardocki took the snap. Dawson's kick hung in the air for what felt like 30 seconds before coming down just over the crossbar, and the new Browns scored their second win. Little was one of the first players on the field in what was a wild celebration.

After the game, Little told reporters he had alerted Dawson to the fact that the clock was running and the Browns didn't have a timeout. Little essentially said that he saw the clock ticking under 20 seconds, sprinted down the bench area towards where Dawson had been kicking in the net, and screamed at Dawson to get on the field.

That didn't go over well with coach Chris Palmer, who thought Little was showing him up by taking credit for the field goal team getting on the field in time. Little said Palmer chewed him out the next day. Palmer told reporters he was aware of the time situation all along and wanted to ensure that the Steelers would have no time left.

By 2001, Little's college head coach, Butch Davis, had taken over for Palmer and Little became a full-time starter. He played both safety positions and had a knack for finding the ball. Little had entered the NFL undrafted because he said teams were concerned about his mental state after the death of his best friend and college teammate, Marlin Barnes.

Little, who grew up with Barnes in the Liberty City section of Miami, had found Barnes and another longtime friend murdered. Little walked away from college and football for a time while grieving. After going undrafted and spending some time with the Dolphins and Saints, Little caught on with the Browns just short of the midway point of the 1999 season. He played for the Browns through 2004, then finished his career with a short stint in Green Bay.

Given that he was such a cerebral player, it's no surprise that Little later got into coaching. He coached at several South Florida high schools before joining the Florida International University staff under Davis in 2017. Maybe someday he'll be in charge of the field goal team.

17 The Imperfect Season

The 2017 Browns played 16 games. They lost all 16.

They lost on two continents. They lost to the Steelers' backups. They twice lost after leading well into the fourth quarter. They followed a 1–15 season by not winning at all.

Rock bottom.

On the final drive of the final game in Pittsburgh, erratic but brave rookie quarterback DeShone Kizer stepped up in the pocket to find a passing lane. He saw Corey Coleman standing basically alone inside the Steelers' 5-yard line. But Coleman dropped the ball, the Steelers won, and there probably couldn't have been a more fitting ending to a winless season and two-year losing project.

The Browns entered that season with no plan at quarterback. They'd drafted Kizer in the second round but believed, correctly, that he wasn't ready. They'd traded for Brock Osweiler but only to acquire a second-round pick; they weren't even sure Osweiler was going to be on the team, but both Osweiler and Cody Kessler got shots to run the first-team offense in training camp.

Myles Garrett, the No. 1 pick in the 2017 Draft and the reward for their 1–15 season in 2016, suffered a high ankle sprain on a freak play in practice just days ahead of the season opener. There were signs that the Browns were on a fast track to no wins, and head coach Hue Jackson seemed incapable of applying the emergency brake.

Kizer was tough, and he had to be. When he dropped back, all that cap space and all those draft picks the Browns had accumulated under Sashi Brown weren't getting open. The Browns' defense was left on the field for too long. Not every game was a blowout, but a bunch of them were. By mid-October, Jackson benched Kizer, saying the rookie needed a week to watch from the sideline and clear his head. In Houston, the Browns got picked apart by Deshaun Watson. Kizer's replacement, Kevin Hogan, had no chance. In late October, the Browns went to London and led the Vikings at halftime before reality set in. Garrett didn't make the trip after suffering a concussion in practice and getting criticized on the team's official radio show by former NFL linebacker Matt Wilhelm for reporting it. The Browns were truly the laughingstock of sports.

Sashi Brown, who'd been put in charge of the roster despite in 2016 never having been a talent evaluator, was fired in December 2017. John Dorsey took over as general manager about six months after being fired by the Chiefs. Brown had loaded up on draft picks and had the Browns in good financial shape for the future, but Haslam couldn't trust Brown to make football decisions. The upcoming picks were too valuable, and the losing had taken its toll on everyone.

Dorsey was around for the final month of the 2017 season. He cut disappointing receiver Kenny Britt on his first day on the job. By the following March, Dorsey traded Kizer. Coleman was traded the next August, and the 2018 Browns started the season with 31 new players. They turned the assets (and losses) Brown had collected into Baker Mayfield, Denzel Ward, Austin Corbett, and Nick Chubb in the 2018 Draft. Ward went to the Pro Bowl, Chubb set the Browns' rookie rushing record, and Mayfield set the NFL record for most touchdown passes by a rookie with 27.

The 2018 Browns went 7–8–1. Jackson was fired at midseason, and the Browns went 5–3 after that. Under Dorsey, the Browns appeared on the path to a bright future. Just 16 months removed from going 0–16, the Browns added Odell Beckham Jr. to that promising group of young players and were chosen for four national TV games in 2019. From unwatchable to must-see TV, the Browns were headed upward. Most of the main characters in their 0–16 story had been removed.

18 The Hall of Fame

Upon returning to the NFL in 1999, the Browns played in the Hall of Fame Game, the annual kickoff to the preseason. They'll probably play in that game again in 2023.

That's when offensive tackle Joe Thomas will be inducted into the Pro Football Hall of Fame. Thomas never missed a game in his 11-year career until a torn triceps muscle in 2017 led Thomas to call it quits. He was a 10-time Pro Bowler and six-time All-Pro.

At 16, the Browns had the fourth-most Hall of Famers as of 2019. The Hall of Fame was established in Canton in 1963, and quarterback Otto Graham became the first Browns inductee in 1965. Graham led the Browns to 10 consecutive championship games in the 1940s and 1950s and was the winning quarterback on four AAFC championship teams and three NFL champions. A seven-time All-Pro and five-time Pro Bowler, Graham was named NFL MVP in 1951, 1953, and 1955.

The Browns have four running backs in the Hall: Jim Brown, Marion Motley, Bobby Mitchell, and Leroy Kelly. The team is represented by three pass-catchers in Canton, wide receivers Dante Lavelli and Paul Warfield and tight end Ozzie Newsome.

Paul Brown, head coach from the franchise's inception in 1946 until 1962, was inducted in 1967. Lou Groza, the franchise's all-time leading scorer as a kicker and also a dominant left tackle, was inducted in 1974. Also in the Hall from the team's early days are defensive end Len Ford, tackle Bill Willis, tackle Mike McCormack, and center Frank Gatski.

The Browns won the AAFC Championships in all four of their years in that league (1946–49), then won the NFL Championship in 1950. They won two more NFL titles in the 1950s, then again in 1964. Jim Brown retired after that 1965 season.

Guard Joe DeLamielleure played much of his career in Buffalo but played his last five seasons with the Browns, and Gene Hickerson opened holes for the likes of Jim Brown and Kelly in two different stints with the Browns, from 1958 to 1960 and 1962 to 1973.

Thomas will be the first Browns player to enter the Hall since Hickerson was inducted in 2007, and he's a near-lock to be the first Browns player inducted the first time he's eligible five years after retirement since Warfield.

In the 2000s, former Browns Clay Matthews, Earnest Byner, Willie McGinest, Eric Metcalf, and Earnest Byner made the modern-era nominees list at various points. McGinest, whose best years came with the Patriots before he played his final three seasons with the Browns, is the NFL's all-time postseason sacks leader. In 2019, Matthews made the semifinalist list for the third time, but he had yet to advance to the finalist round.

The best chance for Matthews, the Browns' all-time sack leader at 62, to make the Hall figures to come down the road as part of the seniors' inductee group. Matthews played 16 of his 19 NFL seasons for the Browns. His 278 games are the most played by a linebacker in NFL history.

The Browns' trade for wide receiver Odell Beckham Jr. in March 2019 probably gave the new-era team its best chance for a Hall of Fame player outside of Thomas. A three-time Pro Bowl pick when the trade was made, Beckham went over 1,000 yards receiving in his first three full seasons before getting traded to the Browns when he was 26. A top athlete with a knack for making the phenomenal catch seem easy, Beckham came to the Browns when Baker Mayfield was beginning his second season and the receiving corps was already better than it had been in a decade.

Alex Mack will one day have a Hall of Fame case, though probably not enough of one. Jamal Lewis has a Hall of Fame case, too. The 2003 AP NFL Offensive Player of the Year went over 2,000 yards that season with the Ravens and over 10,000 for his career. Lewis went over 1,000 yards in seven of the eight full seasons he played, including both of his full seasons with the Browns. He's the only Browns running back besides Jim Brown to rush for more than 1,300 yards in a season.

The leading rusher in Ravens' history finished his career with the Browns in 2009. He helped push the Ravens to the Super Bowl as a rookie in 2000, then missed the next year with a knee injury. He finished his career with 10,607 yards and 58 rushing touchdowns. Through 2018, Lewis ranked 24th on the NFL's all-time rushing yards list and was one of seven players in NFL history to have posted a 2,000-yard rushing season.

19 Metcalf Goes Legend

The best way to become a Browns legend is to help beat the Steelers.

Setting franchise records and providing end-game heroics while doing it ensured that Eric Metcalf will never be forgotten.

On October 24, 1993, Metcalf returned two punts for touchdowns as the Browns beat the Steelers, 28–23. Metcalf took off up the sideline on a 91-yard punt return early in the game to give the Browns a 14–0 lead, then he put the Browns in first place in the AFC Central on a 75-yard return with 2:05 left.

Eric Metcalf celebrates a 90-yard kickoff return for a touchdown in the Browns' January 6, 1990, playoff victory over the Bills. (Mark Duncan/ AP Photo)

On the second, Metcalf cut through traffic, ran to daylight, and kept running until he jumped into the arms of crazed fans in the Dawg Pound, the notoriously wild bleacher section of the stadium. Metcalf had missed most of practice that week with a knee injury but had enough speed burst to get into the open and provide the exclamation point on the game of his life. He also had 53 yards rushing and caught three passes for 18 yards.

Metcalf was listed at 5-foot-10, 188 pounds, and he might not have been that big. The primary reason many fans lamented the infamous "Metcalf up the middle" call was that the running back was at his best on the edges and in the open field. The electric former Texas star was twice named first-team All-Pro and went to three Pro Bowls, mostly for his return ability, but he was also a dangerous pass-catcher out of the backfield. He got almost 200 touches for the 1993 Browns, accounting for more than 1,100 offensive yards in a season that featured his signature game.

Metcalf ran for a career-best 633 yards and six touchdowns as a rookie in 1989. He totaled just six more rushing touchdowns over the rest of his career but remained a dynamic returner and productive pass-catching back. He had at least 47 receptions in five of his six seasons with the Browns.

After leaving the Browns, Metcalf played two seasons for the Falcons before becoming a part-time player and return specialist for the Chargers, Cardinals, Panthers, Redskins, and Packers. Metcalf finished his 13-year career with 31 receiving touchdowns, 12 rushing touchdowns, 10 punt return touchdowns, and two kick return touchdowns.

20 Hue's High Expectations

In fairness to Hue Jackson, even Paul Brown wasn't going to go 8–8 with the rosters the Browns fielded in 2016–17.

But Jackson's two and a half years as head coach of the Browns can be summed up like this. In late 2016, Jackson was talking with reporters about moving forward and learning lessons from a one-win season when he said the Browns weren't going 1–15 again. If that happened, Jackson said, he'd be swimming in Lake Erie.

After the Browns went 0–16 in 2017, he "jumped" in the lake the following summer with dozens of team employees in what became a fundraiser for the Cleveland Browns Foundation. As Jackson wandered in, his bathing suit almost fell off and local TV stations had to be careful with the footage they used that evening.

So, Cleveland got the full Hue Jackson experience.

Jackson had been head coach of the Raiders for one season in 2011. He'd been successful enough as the Bengals' offensive coordinator to become an A-list coaching candidate. After firing Mike Pettine, the Browns wanted an offensive mind and liked his experience.

It turned out Jackson was still stubborn and power-hungry the second time around. The Browns were generally outmanned, but Jackson did little to show he would be part of the solution. Under Jackson the Browns twice lost to the Steelers while the Steelers sat key starters ahead of the playoffs. They led the Ravens 20–0 in the first quarter in 2016 but didn't score again. They didn't win a division game under Jackson until beating the Ravens in overtime in 2018. Their 2017 trip to London was technically a home game and wasn't part of Jackson's 0–20 road record with the Browns, but it did mean his teams suffered blowout losses on two continents.

Even after John Dorsey was hired as general manager in December 2017, Jimmy Haslam insisted that Jackson be given a third year as coach after going 1–31 in his first two. And so another poorly arranged marriage went forward with Dorsey calling the shots and Jackson staying on as head coach for 2018.

Drink Up

The Browns had a sense of humor about their winless 2017 season, at least to an extent. Before the 2018 season they partnered with Anheuser-Busch for the "Victory Fridge" promotion.

Anheuser-Busch placed 10 refrigerators full of Bud Light in Cleveland-area bars, sent some smaller ones to local celebrities and even placed one in the FirstEnergy Stadium pressbox dining area. Each Victory Fridge was closed with a chain and a timelock release.

They would open only once the Browns won a regular season game.

The promotion started in August, giving time for the word to get out and for the bars involved to promise free beer to patrons who came back once the regular season began in September. The Browns rallied in their opener but ended up settling for a bizarre tie vs. the Steelers, then lost a heartbreaker in the final seconds the next week in New Orleans.

But their Week 3 Thursday night home game vs. the Jets ended up being memorable for more than just the free beer it brought a few hundred loyal fans. After starting quarterback Tyrod Taylor left the game with a concussion, No. 1 pick Baker Mayfield entered the game and led the Browns to their first win in 635 days. A late defensive stand led to the unlocking of the Victory Fridges.

Bud Light got a lot of publicity out of the deal. The Browns got a lot of outside attention and might have made a few thirsty fans along the way. And when that win finally came, there was much partying in the streets. Fans danced and chanted "Baker Mayfield" in the streets as they poured out of FirstEnergy Stadium and headed back towards Cleveland's West 6th Street district, where the pouring continued.

As many saw coming, Jackson made it only eight games into 2018. With the Browns 2–5–1, he was fired a day after the Browns got dominated in Pittsburgh. This predictable firing came with a layer few others of its kind had. Later that same day, the Browns also fired offensive coordinator Todd Haley. The in-fighting between Jackson and Haley had reached the point that Dorsey felt it was affecting the locker room and the entire building, so Haley was also pushed out. The Browns made defensive coordinator Gregg Williams the interim head coach and promoted Freddie Kitchens from running backs coach to offensive coordinator, giving Kitchens his first chance to call plays.

Jackson became the sixth consecutive Browns coach to be fired following a loss to the Steelers. All six firings took place between 2008 and 2018. The Steelers have had three head coaches since 1969.

The Browns started seven quarterbacks in Jackson's 40 games. None won more than one game. Tyrod Taylor was 1–1–1. Baker Mayfield and Robert Griffin both were 1–4. Kevin Hogan's only start was a disaster. Josh McCown was 0–3, Cody Kessler was 0–8, and DeShone Kizer was 0–15 before mercifully being traded at the start of his second year in the NFL. The Browns had no business throwing Kizer out there as a rookie starter on a terrible team in 2017, but they did. And they didn't win a game, but Jackson kept his job for 10 more months.

21 Potential Unfulfilled

Josh Gordon was with the Browns from 2012 to '18. At times, he dazzled. But mostly, he disappointed.

Addiction issues cost Gordon a chance at an incredible career. They cost him millions of dollars, too. Maybe $50 million. Maybe that number is too high because Gordon never followed up his breakout 2013 season and never really took a leap as a player. He went from leading the NFL in receiving yards in 2013 to playing in just 11 more games for the Browns over the following five seasons. He was suspended in at least part of every season from 2013 to '18.

With then-coach Pat Shurmur leading the push for more playmakers, the Browns selected Gordon with a second-round choice in the 2012 Supplemental Draft. He was immature and skinny then, but Gordon often made the spectacular seem routine. In 2013 he served a two-game suspension, then crushed the franchise single-season record with 1,646 receiving yards. The Browns played three different quarterbacks that season, and all three knew that their best plan was often to chuck it to Gordon along the sideline.

But Gordon got suspended for all of 2014, a suspension later reduced by a change in the drug policy adopted by the NFL and the NFL Players Association. Gordon's return in 2014 came as the Browns were making a legitimate playoff push, and in his first game back he caught eight passes for 120 yards and the Browns won. But his production and interest level tailed off from there, and he missed the season finale due to team suspension. Then-coach Mike Pettine was neither the first nor the last to wonder if the talent was worth the headaches.

His 2015 suspension was related to breaking terms of his reinstatement when pictures and videos surfaced showing Gordon and Browns teammates drinking alcohol on a flight to Las Vegas not long after the season. Mike McDaniel, then the Browns' receivers coach, was also in those pictures. Gordon and his then-teammates posted those pictures and videos to Instagram.

He was conditionally reinstated in 2016 and allowed to participate in preseason and training camp, but by the time he was eligible for game action he was back in a treatment center.

The stories were already outrageous before Gordon's 2017 return—he went almost three full years between game appearances—and in a magazine article Gordon claimed he'd been involved with hard drugs and that he'd never played an NFL game sober. In a 2015 letter published on *The Cauldron*, Gordon said he hadn't smoked marijuana since before joining the Browns in the summer of 2012.

In 2014, Gordon and Johnny Manziel were spotted bar-hopping in Cleveland on a December Saturday afternoon, not long before they were due at the team hotel the day before a game vs. the Colts. The stories were wild; and while they were believable, they were ever-changing.

In that 2015 open letter, Gordon wrote: "I am not a drug addict. I am not an alcoholic. I am not someone who deserves to be dissected and analyzed like some tragic example or everything that can possibly go wrong for a professional athlete. I have made a lot of mistakes but I am a good person, and I will persevere."

In 2018, he went through the entire offseason program with the Browns for the first time since 2013. But Gordon announced two days before the start of 2018 training camp that he would be away from the team, saying it was part of the plan set forth for his overall mental health and well-being. There was some gray area as to whether the Browns or the NFL had the final call on Gordon returning to the field, but he was activated upon his return and practiced on a limited basis as he dealt with a hamstring issue. He didn't play in the preseason and Hue Jackson said he would be eligible to play but wouldn't start in the season opener.

Through the years, Gordon had a long list of excuses and appeals. He claimed second-hand smoke caused him to test positive. He claimed he thought his drinking ban had expired. A long list of Browns' regimes stood by him through various issues and various absences, all with some sort of false hope that he'd return, stay out of trouble, and be able to help the Browns over the long haul.

It was never going to happen, and after all that it took something as innocuous as a hamstring injury—and the at-this-point-expected unusual circumstances surrounding it—to end things. The night before the Browns left for New Orleans in September 2018, Gordon had injured his hamstring while shooting a personal hype video in the team's indoor fieldhouse. He had permission to be in the facility that night but hadn't been truthful with the team about what he'd been doing, and when he showed up the next day unable to participate in walk-through the Browns kept him off the trip and decided they were finally ready to move on.

That he started his last game with the Browns after Jackson insisted he wouldn't and that his only catch in that game resulted in a touchdown kind of sums up the whole Gordon experience. There were always mixed signals. There was never enough production to deal with the headaches. There was never any kind of guarantee that Gordon would be available for next day, or even the next play.

When the Browns arrived in New Orleans on that Saturday, GM John Dorsey first announced that the team would be releasing Gordon. Within 48 hours, the Browns worked out a trade to send Gordon and a seventh-round pick to the Patriots for a fifth-round pick. Gordon played in 11 games in New England before stepping away from the team in December 2018, just before the NFL announced another indefinite suspension for Gordon under terms of the league's substance abuse policy.

In early 2019, the Patriots extended Gordon a restricted free agent tender, just in case he got sober and got reinstated. As had (too) long been the case in Cleveland, the talent was too much to ignore.

22 One-Hit Wonder

As a college player, Derek Anderson had a bazooka for an arm and a penchant for throwing it to the wrong team. But the arm talent was tantalizing enough for the Ravens to draft Anderson in the sixth round in 2005—and for the Browns to take a shot on Anderson a few months later despite already having a rookie quarterback in Charlie Frye.

In claiming Anderson via waivers from the Ravens at the end of the preseason, the Browns weren't just trying to tweak the Ravens, who thought they'd be able to sneak Anderson through to their practice squad. The Browns thought Anderson had enough arm to eventually become a starting-quality player with additional seasoning. At the very least, he could challenge the defense down the field as a scout-team quarterback in practice.

At the time, Trent Dilfer was the placeholder quarterback. Charlie Frye was a third-round pick in 2005. The Browns were far from convinced Frye was the answer, but he was next in line. Dilfer didn't work out—he thought he was better than he was, and he didn't take the good-guy, high-road route when a bad team inevitably chose to play the rookie—and he was gone by the next season.

Anderson played in four games in 2006, starting three. He helped the Browns to an early December win as an injury substitute, then started the next three games. Heading to 2007, the Browns basically declared an open competition at quarterback between Frye, the fading incumbent; Brady Quinn, the 2007 first-round pick; and Anderson.

Quinn missed a chunk of camp while holding out and never made a real push. The two-man battle was close, but Anderson never really grabbed the job in the preseason. Frye was steady and had developed a rapport with Braylon Edwards, so he was named the starter. But that lasted about half of the first game, and in the second week Anderson claimed the job as his.

He threw for 328 yards and five touchdowns in a wild win over the Bengals. He went on to lead the NFL with 12.7 yards per completion as he had Edwards, Kellen Winslow Jr., and Joe Jurevicius making plays against smaller defensive backs. Anderson beat his old team twice, too. After forcing overtime on a 51-yard Phil Dawson field goal in Baltimore, the Browns won the overtime coin toss and Anderson completed two throws to set up another field goal and seal a wild victory.

That came amid a stretch in which Anderson threw multiple touchdown passes in seven of 10 games, twice posting 300-yard passing games and three times throwing three touchdown passes in a game. He finished the season 10–5 as a starter with 29 touchdown passes and 3,787 yards.

Life changed quickly for Anderson. *Sports Illustrated* followed him to his hometown and his annual football camp. He went to the Pro Bowl. Anderson was a restricted free agent after the 2007 season and the Browns, fearing the Cowboys and potentially others might poach him, signed him to a three-year deal worth $24 million despite already having invested in Quinn.

Anderson went from making $435,000 in 2007 to getting a $7 million signing bonus. He made about $14.5 million over the following two years, which were difficult on and off the field. His play slipped. He was going through a divorce. The constant yo-yo at quarterback caused tension between Anderson and Quinn and affected the whole team. Even after Anderson's big year, he knew that some fans still wanted Quinn to be the Browns' quarterback of the future. He believed some in the organization did, too, and he wasn't afraid to take on a public fight.

Anderson was 3–6 as a starter in 2008 before getting injured, then 3–4 in 2009 after starting the year as a backup. Anderson never again found the magic—or the confidence—he had in 2007. After the 2009 season, the best thing for the Browns was to move on from both Anderson and Quinn. It was the best thing for both players, too.

After spending 2011–17 as Cam Newton's backup in Carolina, Anderson went unsigned in the ensuing offseason and was prepared for retirement. But the Bills called halfway through the 2018 season and brought him in for a workout, and at 35 he made two starts and three appearances when then-rookie Josh Allen was injured. Anderson probably made a good tutor for Allen. Anderson has certainly seen some things and had wildly different experiences at different times during his NFL career.

Through 20 seasons of the new era, he was the only Browns' quarterback to have been named to the Pro Bowl.

23 Bernie, Bernie

For Browns fans born in late 1970s to early 1980s, and to some even before that, Bernie Kosar might be the franchise's most popular player. He's also one of its most important.

That Kosar's popularity remained—and even grew—in the decades after he left the Browns is in part tied to the new franchise's inability to find a dynamic quarterback. Or even a quarterback who lasted more than a couple seasons. But the Kosar-led Browns won, and for the first time in decades they became legitimate Super Bowl contenders.

The face of that winning program was homegrown, relatable, and successful. Kosar was just cool. From his arrival via the 1985 Supplemental Draft, he made the Browns cool—and he helped make them successful. Fans wrote songs about Kosar. They wore his jerseys, bought his posters and believed he'd get the franchise to its first Super Bowl. Kosar always said he only wanted to play for the Browns, and he was the face of the Browns at a time the team was winning and the NFL was becoming the country's most popular pro sport.

He wasn't Otto Graham, who quarterbacked the Browns in 10 championship games. He wasn't Brian Sipe, the franchise leader in passing yards and engineer of 23 game-winning drives. But Kosar was a native Northeast Ohioan. His sidearm delivery was unorthodox, and he wasn't going to scare anyone with his athleticism. But Kosar was smart, accurate, and effective.

Those 1980s Browns were stars in and around Cleveland. And had it not been for the Denver Broncos and a couple cruel bounces, they might have brought Cleveland a Super Bowl. With Kosar, the Browns had gone to the playoffs five straight years, won four division titles, and lost in the AFC Championship Game following the 1986, 1987, and 1989 seasons.

Kosar graduated from the University of Miami in 1985 while still having two years of college eligibility. At the time, early draft entries did not happen. Players either ran out of college eligibility or graduated before being eligible for the NFL. Kosar was smart enough that he had graduated with a double major in finance and economics, and in March 1985, Kosar announced that he was leaving Miami for pro football.

Because he had always wanted—and apparently planned to—play only for the Browns, Kosar waited until the deadline for the regular draft passed to announce that he planned to leave for the NFL. When the Minnesota Vikings, who had traded for the No. 2 pick in 1985, complained, NFL Commissioner Pete Rozelle eventually let Kosar decide if he wanted to be in the regular draft or the Supplemental Draft.

Following what had been the plan all along, Kosar chose the Supplemental Draft. The Browns had traded a bunch of draft picks, including two future first-rounders, to the Buffalo Bills to acquire the top pick in the Supplemental Draft—that was legal at the time—and knew they'd be landing Kosar. The NFL never confirmed that it later changed the Supplemental Draft format because it felt Kosar and the Browns had played the system, but that's basically what happened.

Kosar started his career as a backup, but after Gary Danielson was injured he took over and guided the Browns to the playoffs. From there, the playoffs became the norm and the expectation.

Kosar quarterbacked the Browns in seven postseason games, throwing 15 touchdown passes and 10 interceptions in those games. He threw 64 passes, completing 33 for 489 yards in a double overtime playoff win against the Jets on January 3, 1987. He threw for 356 yards and three touchdowns in the AFC Championship the next year before the Browns lost in gut-wrenching fashion in a moment that lives in infamy as The Fumble.

But Kosar's numbers were rarely spectacular. He won with his brain, and he often clashed with coaches over play-calling and his desire to sometimes call his own shots. He was a 58.8 percent

Bernie Kosar finds an open receiver during a November 1993 game against the Oilers. (Mitchell Layton/Getty Images)

passer in nine years with the Browns, never threw more than 22 touchdowns in a season and never averaged more than 7.9 yards per attempt. Kosar was 53–51–1 as the Browns' starter. He was benched before he was cut in 1993, a move that essentially made Bill Belichick a villain in Cleveland sports lore. The release of Kosar was the lead story on every Cleveland television station and in every Northeast Ohio newspaper for days after it happened.

Belichick would call releasing Kosar "the most difficult decision I've ever been a part of." But Belichick and the Browns' other decision-makers thought his skills were diminishing and that it was time for the franchise to move on. No one knew at the time that the franchise itself would be moving, or that it would be decades before the Browns would find a quarterback to play near the level at which Kosar played.

With 21,904 yards, Kosar ranks third behind Graham and Sipe on the franchise's all-time passing list. With 116 touchdown passes, he's fourth behind Graham, Sipe, and Frank Ryan. His 14 fourth-quarter comeback wins are second only to Sipe's 17.

Kosar immediately joined the Cowboys after being released by the Browns, winning a Super Bowl ring as a backup. He spent three more seasons as a backup with the Dolphins before retiring after the 1996 season.

In the new era his relationship with the team was sometimes complicated, but after being replaced as the color analyst on preseason broadcasts in 2014, Kosar returned in a lesser role a few years later. He lived much of his post-football life in Miami and was actively serving on the University of Miami's board of trustees, but in recent years he's been living in Northeast Ohio.

24 The Lerner Transition

Long before Baker Mayfield beat the Jets in his first NFL game and ended a stretch of 635 days without a victory, the Browns beat the Jets in arguably the most emotional game of the team's new era.

Team owner Al Lerner lost his battle with brain cancer in October 2002. Four days later, the Browns rallied for a 24–21 victory.

At first, the Browns played like an emotionally exhausted team. The game started with the Browns going three-and-out and Santana Moss returning the ensuing punt 63 yards for a touchdown. Less than a minute into the second quarter, a Chad Pennington touchdown pass to Wayne Chrebet made it 21–3.

The Jets held a 21–6 halftime lead before Tim Couch and the Browns started to battle back in the third quarter. Couch got hot, the defense got some stops and the Browns grabbed the momentum.

Couch had one of his best games, completing 32-of-48 passes for 294 yards, two touchdowns and a game-tying two-point conversion pass to Dennis Northcutt. Phil Dawson gave the Browns a lead on a 35-yard field goal with 3:30 left, leaving the Jets plenty of time to try to win or tie the game. But the Jets only got inside the Browns' 30-yard line with 16 seconds left, and their 44-yard try at tying the game was blocked by Courtney Brown.

The Browns improved to 4–4 with the win. That the Browns would later sneak into the playoffs with a 9–7 record—and a 6–2 road record—made that win even more important.

The Browns blew a 17-point lead in their wildcard game at Pittsburgh, and from there little about the team's transition would be easy. Ownership had been transferred to Al Lerner's son,

Randy. The following offseason, CEO Carmen Policy announced he would be stepping away. Policy had been Al Lerner's choice to run the day-to-day operations because of his football and business experience. Al Lerner never liked being in the spotlight; Randy Lerner liked it even less.

The roster had salary-cap issues and lost several veterans in the months after that 2002 season. Couch would only play one more season due to injuries. By the end of the 2004 season Butch Davis was out, and a year after that team president John Collins—the successor to Policy—was gone after an attempted internal power play aimed at then-GM Phil Savage. The Browns were a mess, on and off the field, and that became a recurring theme.

Randy Lerner was 40 when he took over. Most weeks, Lerner would fly in from New York once a week to spend the day in Berea at the Browns' training facility. He had been an investment banker and a football fan, but not a football person. Like his father, he believed ownership should take a background role and hire people to play leading roles. But the failure to hire the right people—and having those people hire the right quarterback—sent the Browns into a tailspin.

After the Browns won 10 games in 2007 then faltered in 2008, Lerner fired both Savage and head coach Romeo Crennel. Randy Lerner had few strong football people in the organization and no one to tell him "no" when it came to Eric Mangini. In late 2009, Lerner had to pay big money—upwards of $25 million, according to some reports—to hire Mike Holmgren to run the Browns. Holmgren had a strong track record as a coach and a pretty bad one as an executive, but he refused to coach the Browns. He hired a bunch of his buddies and fellow clients of agent Bob LaMonte. The Browns continued to bomb. Mangini made it one more year. Holmgren and his crew made it two more.

In 2012, Lerner sold the team to Jimmy and Dee Haslam for $1 billion. The Haslams agreed to pay $600 million up front and

$400 million later, no later than 2016. The sale was completed almost exactly 10 years after Al Lerner's death.

25 For Openers

The Dwayne Rudd Game will forever live in Browns' infamy.

Because it was a season opener, it didn't have quite the magnitude of The Drive, The Fumble, or Red Right 88. But a Browns team that believed it was ready to start making real progress was leading a game with 0:00 on the clock, yet still lost because Rudd had celebrated too early and thrown his helmet across the field.

It was the 2002 season opener. The Browns and Chiefs traded big plays throughout, and the Browns led by 13 midway through the third quarter. But the lead changed hands four times in the final 8:05, and with the Chiefs out of timeouts a 41-yard field goal by Phil Dawson with 29 seconds left should have provided the winning points.

But with the Chiefs at their own 47-yard line and just two seconds left, Rudd blitzed Trent Green and believed he'd recorded the game-clinching sack. Rudd chucked his helmet and strutted towards the west end of the stadium, unaware that Green had flipped the ball to 323-pound Chiefs tackle John Tait before going down. Tait rumbled to the Browns' 25-yard line before being tackled, which would have marked the end of the game had Rudd not been assessed an unsportsmanlike conduct penalty for his helmet toss.

The Chiefs were given an untimed down, and Morten Andersen kicked a 30-yard field goal to give the Chiefs a nearly unexplainable 40–39 victory.

Rudd was a good addition for the Browns when he signed a five-year, $23 million contract in 2001. Linebacker had been a glaring weakness, and his speed and range immediately helped a defense that at the time needed just about all the help it could get. He ended up playing just two seasons with the Browns and one after that unforgettable moment, one that stands as head-scratchingly stupid even among others of its kind.

The Browns finally won a season opener in 2004, Jeff Garcia's first game as Browns' quarterback. The Ravens came to Cleveland heavily favored and with one of the league's best defenses, and defenses dominated most of that day. With the game tied, 3–3, late in the third quarter, Garcia caught Hall of Fame safety Ed Reed cheating up and trying to make a game-changing play. Garcia was able to pop one over Reed's head to Quincy Morgan for what became a 46-yard score, and the Browns went on to win, 20–3.

The next week, Garcia posted a 0.0 quarterback rating and Kellen Winslow Jr. suffered a broken leg late in a loss at Dallas, setting the 2004 season on a downward spiral that led to Butch Davis resigning as head coach late in that season.

Though openers clearly haven't been the only game that's been unkind to the new-era Browns, their inability to win them hasn't exactly set a strong tone for the season ahead. Making their inability to start with a win more frustrating is that the Browns hosted every season opener from their 1999 return until 2010, when they played at Tampa Bay.

Through 20 seasons back in the league, that 2004 game remained the only opener the Browns had won. They tied the Steelers, 21–21, in 2018 in a game as bizarre as the cold and stormy weather in which it was played. The Browns trailed 21–7 in the fourth quarter and tied the game on Josh Gordon's only catch in what became his last game with the Browns. But Zane Gonzalez had his 43-yard field goal attempt in the final seconds of overtime blocked, so the Browns settled for a tie—and coming off an 0–16 season had to find some solace in at least stopping a 17-game losing streak—despite forcing five turnovers by Ben Roethlisberger.

The Browns rallied in Pittsburgh in 2014 but fell just short. Josh McCown thought he was running for a touchdown in 2015 at the Jets, but he got spun into the air and injured. In 2016, the Eagles thought so little of the Browns that they started rookie Carson Wentz despite Wentz having played minimally in the preseason, and in that game Browns starter Robert Griffin III suffered a shoulder injury that caused him to miss most of the rest of the season. The Browns have found various ways to start seasons on various sour notes, but only once did they lose with no time left due to a thrown helmet.

To be 1–18–1 in season openers takes a remarkable amount of bad luck and a similar amount of bad football, which pretty much sums up the first 20 years as a whole.

26 Derailed by Injury

Athletically, Courtney Brown could do it all. But past his first NFL season, the No. 1 pick in the 2000 NFL Draft couldn't stay healthy and couldn't come close to reaching the lofty expectations the expansion-era Browns had for him.

Nicknamed "The Quiet Storm" because of his low-key demeanor, the Browns envisioned Brown eventually becoming a quiet superstar. Brown showed flashes of dominance, starting with his three-sack game in his rookie season as the Browns notched their first win in Cleveland Browns Stadium. The next year, he didn't debut until November because of injury, but had three sacks and scored a touchdown on a fumble recovery as the Browns built a big lead in Chicago in a game they'd later famously gag away.

He played in all 16 games as a rookie, racking up 69 tackles and often showing up in opposing backfields around the quarterback. But he never played a full season again, and once the injuries started, new ones popped up quickly. His 2001 right knee injury required major surgery, and he had surgeries on his left knee in 2002, 2004, and 2006, essentially ending his career.

He dealt with elbow and biceps injuries, too, frustrating and limiting a player who'd been healthy in college. The Browns cut him in 2004, and Brown played one season with the Broncos before calling it a career at 28. Brown had nine sacks in his first 20 professional games, and though he missed five games in 2002 when the Browns made the playoffs, he was an impact player. But after getting six sacks in 13 games in 2003, Brown was limited to two games in 2004 by a foot injury and was cut after that season as the Browns made a regime change.

Over five seasons with the Browns he totaled 17 sacks, six forced fumbles, and six fumble recoveries.

Listed at 285 pounds, a healthy Brown moved like a 220-pound linebacker. At his pro day in 2000, scouts clocked Brown at 4.52 in the 40-yard dash. His vertical leap was 37 inches. He had long arms, a quick first step, and a knack for finding quarterbacks. He'd left Penn State with an NCAA record 33 sacks. In his senior season, he'd been named Big Ten Defensive Player of the Year and was a finalist for the Nagurski, Bednarik, and Lombardi awards.

He ended up missing (51) almost as many NFL games as he played (61). Brown just couldn't stay healthy, and the injuries prevented a gifted player from ever taking his game—or the Browns—to the next level.

27 The Saga of Peyton Hillis

Peyton Hillis was in position to be remembered as an unlikely star with the Browns, a player dismissed by his first team who became a fan favorite and one of the NFL's top rushers in 2010. But instead Hillis is remembered as a player whose fame and productivity were fleeting. He sparred publicly with team officials over his contract, walked out on his teammates hours before a game, and became a distraction rather than a leader after his breakout season.

The story of Hillis was so bizarre that ESPN at one point reported Hillis had told the Browns he was retiring and pursuing a career as a CIA agent. Hillis denied that, claiming someone from the Browns had planted that story as a way to attempt to sabotage his free agency. When it comes to the new-era Browns, just about anything is believable. And after months of Hillis and the Browns sparring, he left via free agency for the Chiefs in 2012.

Hillis fired three different agents during his two seasons with the Browns. In 2010 he ran for 1,177 yards and became so popular that in the offseason he was voted by fans as the cover player for the following year's Madden video game. But in 2011 he played in just 10 games, battled a hamstring injury, missed a game with what he claimed was a case of strep throat, and skipped a hamstring treatment to get married in his native Arkansas. He never won his all-too-public fight with the Browns for a new contract after his big season and instead went on to sign a one-year deal with the Chiefs.

Hillis came to the Browns in March 2010 as a throw-in as the Broncos traded a sixth-round pick and Hillis, then a fullback, to the Browns for Brady Quinn. Both organizations were going through sort of a reset, with the Broncos trying to move past the short Josh McDaniels era and the Browns needing to rid themselves of both Quinn and Derek Anderson after neither emerged as the team's long-awaited answer at the game's most important position.

A year after Hillis departed for Kansas City, Joe Thomas spoke out on Hillis and what Thomas called "a terrible distraction" for the 2011 Browns.

"He crippled our offense," Thomas said. "We were struggling to find anybody to carry the ball with the injuries we had. To have Peyton going through a contract dispute and basically refusing to play, it was a big distraction. More than anything, he was our starting running back and a good player who was supposed to help us become a successful offense. When he's not there and you don't have anybody else to turn to, it makes it hard to win. Beyond the distraction, it's just not being successful."

Listed at 240 pounds, Hillis was a straight-ahead runner. He played fullback and was probably labeled a short-yardage back because that's what he'd mostly been. In college, he was the third option behind the speedy Felix Jones and Darren McFadden, both of whom were first-round picks.

Hillis only had 13 carries the year before he was traded to the Browns. In 2010, he scored a touchdown in each of the Browns' first four games but didn't become the feature back until Week 3, when he ran for 144 yards against the always-rugged Ravens defense. He went on to finish with 11 rushing touchdowns and post five games of 100 rushing yards. He also caught 61 passes and had two receiving touchdowns.

His biggest game came in the Browns' biggest win of that season, a 34–14 win over the Patriots. Hillis ran for 184 yards and two touchdowns in a game that was never really in doubt. Later in the season Hillis had a three-touchdown game against the Panthers.

After one season with the Chiefs he played two seasons with the Giants, mostly as an injury fill-in and short-yardage back. He was cut after the 2014 season with one year remaining on his contract and never played again. Hillis finished his career with 23 rushing touchdowns and three receiving touchdowns.

28 The Dawg Pound

Two of the best cornerbacks in team history played in the 1980s and left a lasting legacy: The Dawg Pound.

It started in training camp in 1985, when raucous crowds greeted the Browns at Lakeland Community College. Hanford Dixon started calling the defense "Dawgs," and the defense would celebrate big plays with barking. By the time the preseason started, Dixon and his position mate, Frank Minnifield, had fans referring to the bleachers at Cleveland Municipal Stadium as The Dawg Pound.

Fans started showing up to the old stadium's wildest section wearing dog masks, chewing on dog bones, and barking in approval of big plays. There was much barking as the Browns were one of the NFL's best teams in the late 1980s. Dixon adopted the nickname "Top Dawg."

The section's most infamous moment came in 1989, when so many batteries and other objects were thrown at the rival Broncos that game officials forced the teams to switch sides in the fourth quarter.

That wasn't the only game that resulted in wild stories involving foreign objects being chucked from the Dawg Pound. Fans threw Milk Bone dog biscuits. Some fans ate them, too. At times over the years they threw snowballs, bottles, and various pieces of food.

As legend has it—more like legends, as in multiple—a group of fans brought in a keg of beer to every game, and shared willingly. The Dawg Pound became such a part of the Browns and the home-field advantage that a bleachers-only Dawg Pound section was built in the new stadium when it opened in 1999. The Browns trademarked "Dawg Pound" and sold season tickets.

When the new-era Browns started the Cleveland Browns Legends program in 2001 to honor some of the franchise's greats, Dixon was inducted in 2003 and Minnifield was honored two years later.

29 Familiar Face

Ray Horton was able to skip some of the paperwork when he was hired as Browns defensive coordinator in 2016.

He already knew the process. He was already on the payroll.

In the rare non-quarterback story that sums up the first two decades of the new era for the Browns, then-coach Rob Chudzinski had hired Horton as defensive coordinator in 2013. Horton signed a four-year deal, but when Chudzisnki was fired at the end of the 2013 season, his whole staff was replaced.

Assistant coaches sign guaranteed contracts with offset language. That essentially means their money is guaranteed, but in the volatile coaching world, change happens often. Not, like, every single year, but coaches bounce around the league, So, if a coach is making $1 million with the Browns on a three-year deal and by the third is fired, he either gets that remaining $1 million or gets the difference if he accepts another job.

When Hue Jackson wanted to hire Horton as defensive coordinator in 2016, he was still under contract with the Browns, even though he'd been working for the Titans. So, the Browns put Horton on that original contract—his exact salary was not public—and basically gave him an extension for two more years instead of a new contract.

And then he got fired again. And again after one season.

After the Browns went 1–15 in the 2016 season, Jackson told the assistant coaches that he wasn't firing any of them. A few days later, he called Horton and told him he wouldn't be back. Gregg Williams replaced Horton as defensive coordinator. In a bit of irony that probably made Horton chuckle, Williams eventually replaced Jackson as interim coach in 2018 when Jackson was fired at midseason.

In the early 2000s, assistant coaches Steve Hagen and Carl Smith both did multiple stints with the Browns under different head coaches. But their contracts had expired before their returns. That's fairly common. Horton coming back to the same job, under the same contract, was not.

30 K2

The story of the new-era Browns can not be told without the story of Kellen Winslow Jr., who's undoubtedly one of the most talented players the Browns have drafted—and one of the most disappointing.

Winslow's story encompasses it all: questionable drafting, bad injury luck, wild off-field distractions, and brief glimpses of talent leading to winning.

Too brief. Winslow broke his leg in his second game while trying to recover a meaningless onside kick. The next offseason, he nearly died in a motorcycle accident that cost him millions and probably cost him the chance to ever reach his full on-field potential. Winslow came back and had two big seasons. Along the way, he also acquired two staph infections. In 2008, he was suspended for criticizing the team over his second staph infection. In 2009, he was traded to the Buccaneers.

It's hard to know if Winslow ever got back near 100 percent health. He often couldn't practice due to swelling in the knee he injured in the motorcycle accident, and he sometimes would spend days after games basically unable to get off the couch. The Browns would sometimes send tight ends coach Alfredo Roberts to Winslow's house to go over game plans and video corrections so Winslow could keep his knee properly iced.

Going back to the beginning, Winslow was lost two games into his rookie season after being injured late in a game at Dallas. Despite Jeff Garcia posting a 0.0 quarterback rating that day, the Browns were trying to recover an onside kick late and instead lost their first-round pick for the season. The Browns had moved up one spot in the 2004 Draft to take Winslow, allowing Ben Roethlisberger to slip to the Steelers.

After the May 2005 motorcycle accident, Winslow had a lengthy hospital stay and missed the entire season. Due to the wreck, Winslow was in violation of a "dangerous activities" clause in his rookie contract, leading the Browns to withhold a $2 million bonus he was due in 2005. The Browns later redid Winslow's contract. Clauses and bonuses were added to allow Winslow to recoup most of the money he'd lost if he got healthy and returned to help the Browns.

In 2006, he did. Winslow was still a good player, and sometimes a game-changer. In his first full season, 2006, he tied the franchise record with 89 receptions. The next year he caught 82 passes for 1,106 and went to the Pro Bowl after playing with the best offense of the team's new era. But in 2008 he only played in 10 games, dealt with a staph infection, and was suspended for a game after publicly criticizing the team regarding its handling of the infection. The next year, Eric Mangini traded him before he ever had to deal with him.

Winslow was able to stay healthy enough to be a full-time player for three seasons with the Buccaneers. His 12 touchdowns in Tampa Bay topped the 11 he scored in parts of four seasons with the Browns. He bounced around the league late in his career, and three years after playing his last game with the Jets in 2013, he entertained thoughts of a comeback but never signed a contract. He caught 469 career passes for 5,236 yards and 25 touchdowns.

In 2018 and '19, an avalanche of accusation and charges landed Winslow in jail. For offenses alleged to have taken place over a period of almost 20 years, Winslow was charged with multiple counts of sexual assault, kidnapping with intent to commit rape, burglary, and rape, along with many other felonies and misdemeanors. His trial was set to commence in summer 2019.

31 Chasing Baker

After being fired by the Chiefs in the summer of 2017, John Dorsey ran a one-man scouting operation out of his Kansas City–area basement during the following football season.

Dorsey's Monday-Friday routine rarely changed. He'd go to church, go to the gym, then spend the entire afternoon watching film. He figured he'd get another shot to be a general manager, sooner rather than later, and Dorsey was going to be ready when that opportunity came.

From Kansas City, Dorsey could reach Kansas, Kansas State, Missouri, and Arkansas in a relatively easy drive. Campuses in Oklahoma and Iowa weren't much farther. So Dorsey's Saturday routine started with hopping in the car and attending games so he could see NFL prospects in person.

By the time Dorsey accepted the job as general manager of the Browns in December 2017, the Browns were on the verge of clinching the No. 1 pick in the 2018 Draft. With Deshaun Watson, the injured Houston Texans were fading fast, too, and the Browns held the Texans' picks in both the first and second rounds. Dorsey is no dummy; he called the treasure trove of picks a big reason why he accepted the Browns job.

He didn't say publicly that he'd long been working, or that he'd long been drawn to the energy and attitude of Oklahoma quarterback Baker Mayfield, who completed better than 70 percent of his passes over his final two college seasons and won the Heisman Trophy in 2017. Dorsey watched Mayfield rise from two-time walk-on to household name in the football world, and he also had watched in person that day at Kansas when Mayfield, angered that Kansas players wouldn't shake his hand, had made an obscene gesture to the Kansas sideline for which Mayfield would later be briefly suspended.

In early 2017, Mayfield had been arrested on public intoxication and disorderly conduct charges in Fayetteville, Arkansas. Basically, he'd had too much to drink and was causing a scene, and when police approached Mayfield near a food truck he unsuccessfully tried to get away. He later pled guilty to the charges, paid fines, and performed community service.

But the arrest stuck with him as his profile grew, and when Mayfield entered his first formal meeting with Dorsey and the

Browns at the 2018 NFL Scouting Combine, it was the first topic of discussion.

"I walk in the room, and the first thing [Dorsey] said was, 'I hear you like food trucks,'" Mayfield said. "Obviously, John Dorsey has a reputation of not only knowing football but also being himself and not really caring what everybody else thinks. So I have respect for that.

"Going into that meeting I was laughing when he said that. Not only was it pretty funny to hear that from him but it kind of

Baker Mayfield throws a 51-yard touchdown to Jarvis Landry while under pressure from Panthers defensive end Wes Horton during a December 2018 game in Cleveland. (David Richard/AP Photo)

lightened the mood a little bit. All of those meetings are so uptight. Now, it's a good memory. A good first to have."

Mayfield went on to start 13 games for the Browns as a rookie. The Browns won seven games after winning four in the previous three years, and Mayfield set an NFL rookie record with 27 touchdown passes. The Browns went forward thinking they'd finally found their franchise quarterback.

Before the 2018 Draft, Dorsey and the Browns' top decision-makers and coaches flew on Jimmy Haslam's private plane to three places: Norman, Oklahoma, to meet and work out with Mayfield; Los Angeles, for similar meetings with USC quarterback Sam Darnold and UCLA quarterback Josh Rosen; and Laramie, Wyoming, for a private workout with Wyoming quarterback Josh Allen. All included personal time with the quarterbacks and their families.

It was during that trip that Mayfield essentially locked up his status atop the team's draft board. Though Dorsey didn't often say that around the building because didn't want to shade anyone else's thinking—and didn't really trust coach Hue Jackson to not share it externally—Dorsey had his mind made up.

"Personally, I knew in my gut when we left the workout in Norman," Dorsey said. "But when you make a decision this large, you want to have unanimous consent in the building. You don't want to set the stage or alter anything. You want to hear unbiased opinion from everybody, so that's why I kept it as pure as I possibly could."

Dorsey was drawn to Mayfield's arm strength, his accuracy, and his release. But he'd also seen Mayfield on game days, in huddles, and interacting with teammates.

"I think he was in the top three stastically in all the major categories in college football," Dorsey said. "He had the tools. And when you watched his teammates galvanize to him at certain parts of the game, that told me he had at least a little bit of that 'it' factor."

Mayfield would later say that he didn't know Dorsey had long been lurking. But Dorsey did know that Mayfield had soy sauce on his hoodie when the police placed him in handcuffs, and as time passed, Mayfield could laugh at that being their first conversation point.

"I didn't know that he had come to multiple [Oklahoma] games and all that," Mayfield said. "Obviously I had known that we had a decent amount of scouts at some of our games, but I didn't know specifics. And I wasn't worried about that. I had told myself that if I played well enough and I took care of business that all the rest would fall into place.

"But knowing later what games he was at and certain things that happened, looking back it's pretty interesting. When he says we first talked about food trucks, that's absolutely true."

32 Big Ben

For Browns fans, the most disturbing part of the first two decades of the team's new era might not be that Joe Thomas played for six different head coaches and never played in a playoff game. It might not be all the misses in the draft and total whiffs at quarterback. It might not even be that starting in 2008, six consecutive Browns coaches have been fired following losses to the Steelers. Or that a long snapper was the first player drafted by the new-era Browns to be named to a Pro Bowl.

It might be that the winningest quarterback in what's now called FirstEnergy Stadium plays for the Steelers, not the Browns.

Twenty years in to the new era, Roethlisberger had 11 victories in the Browns' new stadium. The winningest Browns' quarterback there is Derek Anderson, who has 10. Joe Flacco, who quarterbacked the Ravens from 2008 to 2018, has eight wins in Cleveland. Only one Browns quarterback is in the top three! The No. 1 pick of the Browns the year they returned to the league, Tim Couch, won seven games in Cleveland Browns Stadium as a starter including the new team's first home win, 23–20, over the Steelers on September 17, 2000. Cleveland-area native Brian Hoyer is next with six wins in the new stadium in 2013–14.

Couch's last year with the Browns was 2003. The Steelers drafted Roethlisberger in 2004, and through 2018 Roethlisberger was 22–2–1 as a starter against the Browns. He also came off the bench in a 2015 game as an injury replacement and threw for 379 yards and three touchdowns as the Steelers rolled to a 30–9 victory. He didn't start due to injury concerns, but apparently he was fine.

The list of Browns quarterbacks Roethlisberger has beaten as a starter is a lengthy one. For some fans, it might be a disturbing one. Jeff Garcia was first. As of this writing, Baker Mayfield was most recent. In between were Charlie Frye, Derek Anderson, Bruce Gradkowski, Colt McCoy, Seneca Wallace, Thaddeus Lewis, Jason Campbell, Brian Hoyer, Austin Davis, Cody Kessler, and DeShone Kizer.

Anderson and the Browns had the Steelers on the ropes in 2007, leading 28–24 in the closing minutes. Browns linebacker Willie McGinest had Roethlisberger wrapped up for what looked to be a sack, but he shook McGinest off and ran to convert a third-and-9—the fourth third down the Steelers converted in that fourth quarter. Two plays after stiff-arming McGinest on that run, the Steelers scored to take the lead on a Roethlisberger pass to Heath Miller. The Browns eventually missed a 52-yard field goal to tie in the closing seconds. Both teams finished 10–6; the Steelers won the division by virtue of their season sweep. The Browns missed the playoffs by one game.

Though that game was the most hurtful to the Browns' playoff chances, perhaps the most deflating near-miss vs. Roethlisberger had come 12 months before in Cleveland. The Steelers slogged through three quarters before Roethlisberger engineered fourth-quarter touchdown drives of 87, 79, and 77 yards, respectively, capping the last with a touchdown via impromptu shovel pass to Willie Parker while Kamerion Wimbley was attempting to take Roethlisberger down by his left arm. The Steelers converted all six of their third-down attempts in that fourth quarter.

Roethlisberger is from Findlay, in Northwest Ohio. Though he always said he was more of a 49ers and Joe Montana fan growing up than a Browns fan, he'd later say he took it personally that the Browns passed on him in the draft. He was just five games into his NFL career—and in just his third start—when he beat the Browns for the first time. He didn't lose a game to the Browns until 2009, and he's still unbeaten vs. the Steelers' closest geographical rival in games played in Pittsburgh.

A few weeks before that 2004 Draft, head coach Butch Davis and Pete Garcia, then the Browns' top personnel executive, summoned backup wide receivers Frisman Jackson and Andre King to the team's facility early on a Monday morning. They were asked to grab their football shoes and be ready "within an hour," King recalled, to be on owner Randy Lerner's jet. The Browns were flying to Oxford for a private workout with Roethlisberger, and they were bringing their own receivers.

After about 90 minutes of throwing, Davis, Garcia, Terry Robiskie (then the offensive coordinator), and Steve Hagen (then the quarterbacks coach) spent time talking Xs and Os with Roethlisberger. Jackson and King were driven back to the local airstrip and flown back to Cleveland.

"We were back by lunch," King recalled.

Of the workout, Jackson would later say that "five minutes in, it was obvious that Ben could throw the hell out of the football." One painfully interesting sidenote is that Garcia suffered a broken nose during the workout after one particularly juiced-up pass deflected off the hands of its intended receiver and hit Garcia in the face before he could get his hands up to protect himself.

After taking King and Jackson back to Cleveland, Lerner's plane then returned to Oxford, where it picked up the Browns' contingent and flew to Raleigh, North Carolina, for a similar meeting and workout with Philip Rivers, who had just completed his college career at North Carolina State. Rivers ended up going No. 4 in that draft, then landed with the Chargers after a trade involving Eli Manning. The Browns made a trade, too, going up one spot to No. 6 to select tight end Kellen Winslow Jr., who'd played under Davis at the University of Miami. Roethlisberger went to the Steelers at No. 11.

Garcia would later say "it was very, very close" on the team's draft board between Winslow and Roethlisberger.

"We thought long and hard about picking Ben," Garcia said. "He was right up there with [Winslow] and anyone else we considered. We graded him as a difference-maker. In the end, we went with a difference-maker at a different position and a guy we knew a little bit better than we knew Ben."

Of all the draft misses by the new-era Browns, the argument could be made that none were more hurtful—or more painful to fans—than the Browns picking Winslow over Roethlisberger.

33 Jerome Harrison's Huge Game

On December 20, 2009, in Kansas City, a bad Browns team trailed a bad Chiefs team in a game that was on its way to being a forgettable and necessary step to both teams just completing their respective seasons.

Then Jerome Harrison started bouncing off of Chiefs players. And making them miss. And not only did a 24–13 second-quarter lead for the home team evaporate in what became a wild game, but Harrison turned in one of the best rushing performances in NFL history.

Harrison rushed for 286 yards, breaking franchise and stadium records. The Browns went on to win, 41–34, with the winning margin coming on a 28-yard run by Harrison in the final minute. As Harrison broke through the first layer of the Chiefs' defense on that run, Browns coach Eric Mangini was screaming for Harrison to go down intentionally. The game was tied, but the Chiefs were out of timeouts and Mangini wanted the Browns to kill the clock and win on a field goal in the closing seconds.

The Chiefs couldn't stop Harrison, though, and he wasn't going to stop himself.

His big day really got rolling on the opening drive of the second half, when he took off on a 71-yard touchdown run to give the Browns the lead. He scored again early in the fourth quarter from 12 yards out. Harrison had 12 carries for 73 yards in the first half; he ended up carrying the ball 34 times at an average of 8.4 yards per pop.

As of 2018, Harrison's 286-yard rushing day still stood third in NFL history behind Adrian Peterson's 296 yards for the Vikings vs. the Chargers in 2007 and the 295 yards Jamal Lewis got against the Browns in 2003.

To set any type of rushing record with the team Jim Brown put on the map puts a player in pretty elite company. A fifth-round pick in 2006 who'd been mostly a backup until the Browns placed Lewis on injured reserve two weeks earlier, Harrison came into that game averaging 3.4 yards per rush but hadn't gone over 35 yards since his 121-yard performance 11 weeks earlier. At the time, he had just one prior rushing touchdown in his career.

Brown still holds three of the top 30 individual rushing games in NFL history. His 237 yards vs. the Rams in 1957 and vs. the Eagles in 1961 are part of a four-way tie at No. 20, and his 232 yards vs. the Cowboys in 1963 is tied for 29th with another performance by a Browns player, Hall of Famer Bobby Mitchell vs. the Redskins in 1959.

Brown was at the game in Kansas City, watching from the Browns' owners suite, and greeted Harrison afterwards.

"Harrison is a young man I respect a lot," Brown said. "I talk to him often. I've been in his corner. I respect his talent and I'm happy for him. Seeing his work pay off, that's much greater than me holding on to a record."

Harrison was traded to the Eagles the next season after averaging just 2.9 yards per carry on 31 rushes. He finished the 2010 season there, then played briefly for the Lions. Upon being traded back to the Eagles in 2011, a physical revealed a mass on his brain that would later be identified as a benign tumor that required immediate surgery. He went through a multi-year process of dealing with various medical issues but survived, and as of 2018 he was learning to walk again.

34 Limitless Potential

Myles Garrett is into poetry, dinosaurs, and crushing quarterbacks. On and off the field, he's different.

Does superstardom lie ahead? If Garrett can stay healthy and continue to add to his pass-rush moves, it sure looks that way.

The No. 1 pick in the 2017 Draft has all the physical gifts. His muscles have muscles. He has a quick first-step and range to close on unsuspecting quarterbacks. At 23, Garrett recorded 13.5 sacks in his second season, the second-highest single-season total in Browns history behind Reggie Camp's 14 in 1984.

Garrett led all NFL defensive linemen in number of snaps played in his second season. Though that's not ideal, he didn't want to leave the field. He can rush inside and outside, and with his closing speed he stands to rack up the sacks in the years ahead if he continues to refine his game.

A freak practice injury ahead of the 2017 opener left Garrett with a high ankle sprain, an injury that can linger. He didn't make his NFL debut until October, then later that month suffered a concussion and missed more time. It wouldn't be accurate to say his rookie season was a lost season, but he missed a significant amount of time and often played at less than 100 percent.

Garrett recorded a sack as an inside rusher on his first career snap vs. the Jets, displaying the kind of rare burst and finishing ability that made him the No. 1 pick. He finished his rookie season with seven sacks in 11 games.

A rare athlete with long arms and light feet, he recorded a 41-inch vertical jump and was timed at 4.64 seconds in the 40-yard dash while weighing 272 pounds at the NFL scouting combine.

Myles Garrett celebrates after sacking Ben Roethlisberger. (Jeff Haynes/AP Photo)

Leading up to the 2017 Draft, Garrett conducted only one private workout, for the Browns. And it was a brief one. He knew, the team knew, and though the Browns still needed a quarterback, they weren't passing on Garrett.

"There was one moment when I realized, like, 'Whoa, this kid is legit,'" Joe Thomas said. "There was a clip that was shown in the team meeting. It was a screen play that went opposite of where Myles was lined up. The ball was snapped and Myles ran up the field 10 yards or so, behind the quarterback, and the quarterback dumps the ball off to the running back.

"Myles is probably 15 yards behind the running back when the ball is caught. And no one is tackling in practice, so the back kind of keeps running, but so does Myles. And you see Myles kind of click into that next gear and all of a sudden those strides get longer, they get more powerful, and about 60 yards down the field he runs to and then past that running back. The coaches showed that play making a point about hustle and intensity. But it was just remarkable to watch that talent, that second gear. He was as fast as any defensive back I've ever seen and he's 270 pounds.

"He's just chiseled. It's amazing how strong he is. Myles came in as a rookie and he was just freakishly strong. He has all the tools. He's one of the most explosive guys I've seen."

Garrett became a star in his freshman season at Texas A&M, when he led the team with 11.5 sacks, an SEC freshman record, and 14 tackles for loss. Even two years before he was draft-eligible, some predicted then that he'd be the top pick in 2017. Garrett comes from an athletic family. His mother and sister were college track stars. His older half-brother, Sean Williams, was a first-round pick in the NBA in 2007 before his career was sidetracked by off-court issues.

The Browns found no issues with Garrett. He keeps to himself, and after that disappointing rookie season he came back stronger, in better shape, and focused on reaching his potential. He never talks about specific individual goals, but he insinuates that they're ridiculously high.

"My brother was an example of what not to do," Garrett told *Sports Illustrated* during his college career. "The weed, it's a distraction. A lot of things can be distractions—girls, other drugs, fame, and ego. I don't want anything to distract me from my main goal, which is going to the NFL and being the best defensive lineman, the best defensive player who ever played."

Garrett played a little basketball, too. Playing in a pickup basketball game at a Cleveland-area rec center shortly after his second season, Garrett shattered a backboard. On the football field, he looks like a player capable of eventually shattering the franchise sack record, 62 by Clay Matthews.

35 The Toe

The Browns' all-time leading scorer grew up in Ohio and played a staggering 21 years with the team, starting with the organization's inception in 1946.

They don't make 'em like Lou Groza anymore. A straight-on kicker, Groza wore black high-top shoes and big shoulder pads for his other job. As an offensive tackle he was a six-time All-Pro and was named NFL Player of the Year by the *Sporting News* in 1954.

Groza played for the Browns from 1946 to 1967. He was a kicker only from 1961 on after suffering an injury, and he retired after making 264 field goals and logging 1,608 career points. He was named to the Pro Bowl every year but one in the 1950s and was an All-Pro every season from 1952 to '55. The Martins Ferry, Ohio, native was elected to the Pro Football Hall of Fame in 1974.

A key member of four championship teams in the All-America league, Groza scored 1,349 of his points in the NFL, which still ranked 15th at the time of his death. He led the NFL in field goals made in five different seasons and played on nine Browns teams that reached NFL championship games, winning four. His 16-yard field goal in the final seconds gave the Browns a 30–28 win over the Los Angeles Rams in the 1950 NFL title game.

The address of the Browns' team headquarters and practice facility is 76 Lou Groza Boulevard in Berea, where Groza lived, which is about 15 minutes southwest of the site of FirstEnergy Downtown Cleveland. That facility opened in 1991 and has been renovated multiple times during the team's new era.

Phil Dawson, the first full-time kicker of the team's new era, is second on the scoring list. Dawson didn't double at tackle for the Browns but he'd grown up playing other positions and brought that mentality to his job. A native Texan, Dawson adapted to Cleveland's unfavorable and unpredictable weather conditions and delivered some of his biggest kicks in blizzards. Dawson is the Browns' new-era leader with 305 field goals, from 1999 to 2012, but with 1,271 total points he's well behind Groza.

Dawson was a student both of his craft and of football history. He had a deep respect for Groza, who died in 2000 at 76. Dawson maintained a relationship with the Groza family long after Lou Groza's death.

The next two kickers on the scoring list are Don Cockroft (1968–1980) with 1,080 points and 216 field goals; and Matt Bahr (1981–89), who had 143 career field goals and 677 points. Matt Stover was good with the Browns from 1991 to '95 but is best remembered for his clutch kicks with the Ravens after the team moved to Baltimore.

Cockroft, a third-round pick who kicked for the Browns for 13 seasons, might be best remembered for one he didn't get to kick in the infamous Red Right 88 game vs. the Raiders in the 1980 playoffs. Down 14–12 in the final minute, Brian Sipe's pass intended for Ozzie Newsome was intercepted by Mike Davis and the Browns were upset. In brutally cold and windy conditions, Cockroft had previously missed two field goals and had an extra-point attempt blocked.

Cockroft ranks No. 3 on the Browns' scoring list. Jim Brown is fourth with 756 points; his 126 career touchdowns still ranked in the top 10 in NFL history through the 2018 season.

Brown is followed by Bahr, Leroy Kelly (540), Stover (480), and Gary Collins (420). Dante Lavelli (372) and Ray Renfro (330) round out the top 10.

After Dawson, the leading scorer of the new era is kicker Billy Cundiff, who kicked for the Browns in parts of three seasons and made 49 mostly forgettable field goals in 61 tries en route to 211 points. With 172 points, Braylon Edwards is the top non-kicking scorer of the new era.

36 Streak Almost Snapped

By an unofficial count, Joe Thomas played 10,363 consecutive snaps before the triceps injury that led to his retirement following the 2017 season. The No. 3 pick in the 2007 NFL Draft became the immediate starter at left tackle and didn't give the job up for more than a decade.

But there were a couple of times the streak was in danger, and one of the times had nothing to do with injury or exhaustion. Late in an October 2014 game against the Steelers—the Browns were actually winning by a bunch—then-coach Mike Pettine sent a backup tackle named Vinston Painter into the huddle to replace Thomas. Gently, Thomas told Painter to take a hike. And hike back to the sideline Painter did.

It was never the style of Thomas to talk about the streak, or to talk about himself at all. He was humble and self-deprecating in addition to being insanely reliable and consistent. But the streak meant something to him. Earlier in that game, Pettine had seen the Browns lose Alex Mack to a broken leg. Mack had never previously missed a snap since being drafted in 2009.

Pettine didn't want to take any chances with Thomas, but Thomas wanted to keep playing. He hadn't taken himself out previously, and that wasn't going to change.

He'd been close. In the 2012 season finale, a 24–10 loss with a third-stringer playing quarterback and the head coach a day away from getting fired, Thomas tore the lateral collateral ligament in his knee. He knew it, too, but he stayed in the game.

"I heard the pop and was in pain," Thomas said in 2017. "I had to really try to test it a little bit to see if I could continue to play. Other than that, I've just had your garden-variety pain and anguish that you go through in certain games and with certain injuries, but I think that is probably the one that sticks out the most in my head as far as ones that were close to not knowing if I was going to be able to play."

Garden-variety pain and anguish. Ten consecutive losing seasons. Third-string quarterbacks and wholesale organizational changes. Still, there was Thomas. Playing, leading, battling through the change and the bruises and the sprains. He's almost certain to be a first-ballot Hall of Famer.

Thomas played for two owners and six head coaches. Thomas would often say that when other teams reconvened each spring for formal workouts and light practices now known as organized team activity sessions, teams that had kept their core players and coaches intact would have the chance to clean up areas in which they'd struggled the previous season, install new wrinkles to plays they already had seen work and concentrate on little things such as third-down and red-zone efficiency.

The Browns players and coaches were just introducing themselves.

Thomas took notes on opposing pass-rushers. He tutored young linemen on both sides of the ball. In 2015, the Browns almost traded him to Denver. He let it be known that he wanted to stay and see things through.

In 2016, with Sashi Brown leading a full teardown of a bad roster, trading Thomas made sense. But Brown and Hue Jackson said they wanted Thomas to stay, and Thomas appreciated that. He said he didn't treasure the streak as an exact number, but rather a symbol of how he wanted to be remembered. Long before the torn triceps injury, he'd openly discussed the measures he had to take to keep playing and would often say he recognized that football wouldn't be forever.

But while he was there, he certainly wasn't letting Vinston Painter take the streak away.

"Throughout my career there have been instances where guys take themselves out of a game," Thomas said. "Maybe they don't feel good. To that I say, 'I hardly ever feel good. But it's my job to go out there and play.' Unless you actually can't do it or unless the guy behind you is going to do it better than you can, I think you should be out there playing.

"I think it was just something that was ingrained in me when I was a little kid. It was just all about being out there to help your teammates and doing everything you can to help the team win. Fighting through pain and adversity. I never really considered not going out there and giving my all because I always felt that the team and my teammates relied on me to be out there. No matter what the conditions were or what situation the team was in, I always felt that it was my job to be out there."

37 The Trade For Odell Beckham

For more than a year, Browns general manager John Dorsey entertained the thought of trading for All-Pro wide receiver Odell Beckham Jr.

Dorsey had prioritized the wide receiver position in his first offseason with the Browns, and before the start of the 2018 league year he traded for Jarvis Landry, a Pro Bowl wide receiver with the Dolphins who's also one of Beckham's best friends. Dorsey had a long-standing relationship with Giants general manager Dave Gettleman, and the Browns that spring held four of the first 35 picks in the draft.

The timing seemed right if the Giants were ready to bail on Beckham and go into a bit of a rebuilding phase. Longtime Giants quarterback Eli Manning was 37 at the time and entering his 15th NFL season. But Beckham was just 25 and had gone to the Pro Bowl in each of his first three seasons, and it made more sense for the Giants to sign him and keep him. The initial Browns-Giants conversations never got out of the conversation phase.

Beckham at the time was coming off a broken leg that had ended his 2017 season after just four games and was headed into the fifth and final season of his rookie contract. He'd played at a level that made him deserving of becoming one of the NFL's best wide receivers, but he'd also had on and off-field incidents that reeked of immaturity and rubbed some in the Giants' organization the wrong way.

But Beckham was undoubtedly a star on and off the field, and his on-field production was worth a few headaches or distractions. In August 2018, the Giants signed Beckham to a five-year contract worth $65 million in guaranteed money and up to $90 million in total. Though Landry kept talking about the Browns continuing to pursue Beckham, the contract made it unlikely that the Giants would trade him—and made it so their salary cap would take a significant hit if it did.

In early 2019, Gettleman said on the record that the Giants didn't sign Beckham to trade him.

But on March 12, 2019, the Giants did trade him. In a deal that came together quickly—and was made five days after the Browns and Giants had agreed on another trade that involved the Browns trading guard Kevin Zeitler for edge rusher Olivier Vernon—the Browns sent their 2019 first-round pick (no. 17 overall), young safety Jabrill Peppers, and a late third-round pick (No. 95 overall) to the Giants for Beckham.

"We spoke it into existence," Landry would later say.

Dorsey insisted that the two trades were made separately even though they ultimately became official as one trade. Rumors about the Giants talking a potential Beckham trade with the 49ers and other teams had led Dorsey to call Gettleman and ask, one more time, if he truly was available. With the Browns' key decision-makers gathered in the draft room to plot their strategy for the second and third waves of free agency, their attention instead turned to what would become one of the biggest trades in team history—and certainly the biggest in nearly 35 years since the Browns had traded to secure the Supplemental Draft rights to Bernie Kosar.

By 4:00 PM that day, Dorsey started to believe the Browns would be able to finalize the deal. It took several hours after that to actually complete it, with those in the Browns' draft room sharing hugs and handshakes over what started as a crazy idea becoming reality.

"It was a hypothetical that sometimes you can plan for, but you can plan for stuff that 99 percent of the time does not transpire," Dorsey would later say. "This just so happened to be that one percent that your planning actually paid off."

Indirectly, the Browns have the Steelers to thank for acquiring Beckham. The trade came on the heels of the drama caused by Steelers All-Pro wide receiver Antonio Brown, whose bizarre behavior basically forced the Steelers to trade him to the Raiders for third and fifth-round picks. The Giants didn't want their already strained relationship with Beckham to get worse, nor did they want Beckham to publicly ask out or act out against the team the way Brown had done. Two days after the Raiders got Brown for that discount price, the Browns got Beckham.

Dorsey's relationship with Gettleman helped get it done. Gettleman trusted that Dorsey would keep conversations private, and because Dorsey had been persistent in asking about Beckham, Gettleman knew Dorsey was serious and wasn't just fishing for information. ESPN later reported that Gettleman only got "reluctant approval" from Giants owner John Mara, but Beckham's clashes with Giants (and former Browns) coach Pat Shurmur had led Mara to sign off on the deal.

Fifteen months after barely averaging two touchdowns per game in an 0–16 season, the Browns had their quarterback in Baker Mayfield and Mayfield had top-tier options in Beckham and Landry. For the first time in over a decade, the Browns had a season-ticket waiting list. Beckham was in Europe when the trade was made. He knew something was happening when he saw Gettleman calling. His first call after that was to his mother. The second was to Landry, who he'd known since high school. Beckham and Landry starred together at LSU.

Odell Beckham Jr. poses with his Browns jersey during his introductory news conference on Monday, April 1, 2019, in Berea, Ohio. (Ron Schwane/AP Photo)

"I would tell Browns fans to get ready for some of the most exciting times of their lives," Beckham said on a team-owned TV program shot on his first day inside the facility. "We want everybody there. I want to be able to give these people the most excitement you can possibly have and win, obviously. I'm coming as the best version of myself with the goal to be the very, very best player I can be for the Cleveland Browns."

38 Sashi's Brief Stint

After going 3–13 in 2015 with a team that was essentially directionless and had few answers at key positions, owner Jimmy Haslam did what he'd done two years prior and cleaned house, this time firing head coach Mike Pettine and general manager Ray Farmer. He followed that by surprisingly promoting Sashi Brown from general counsel to head of the football operation.

A few days later, the Browns hired former baseball general manager Paul DePodesta as their chief strategy officer. The Browns were going to an analytics-driven front office that was going to be different in a lot of ways from its NFL counterparts.

The first was that the Browns weren't immediately going to be trying to win. They never publicly used the word "tanking," but the Browns were undertaking a multi-year rebuilding project that would start by essentially taking things down to the studs. The Browns cut veterans, traded back in the draft to acquire more picks, and set out on a plan to acquire enough picks to acquire five drafts worth of players over three years.

Hue Jackson took the job, anyway. About two weeks after Brown and DePodesta started in their new roles, the Browns hired

Jackson as their eighth full-time head coach of the new era. Jackson had previously been the head coach of the Raiders for one season and had gotten back onto the radar through his work as offensive coordinator of the Bengals. The Browns hadn't hired a head coach with previous NFL head coaching experience since Eric Mangini in 2009.

Jackson knew that a head coach's job was to win. In his defense, he was given no chance to do it. Jackson and the front office mostly played nice for the first year, but things got ugly in the second year when Jackson kept making promises that the Browns were ready to win and compete and the 2017 results didn't back that up. After a loss in London at the midpoint of the 2017 season, Jackson took on the front office publicly. A few days later, the front office kept Jackson from trading for quarterback A.J. McCarron.

So, the Browns had taken an unconventional route to getting back to a good, old-fashioned power struggle.

ESPN would later report that Brown and DePodesta preferred to hire Sean McDermott, then the defensive coordinator in Carolina, but were overruled by the Haslams, who wanted Jackson. When the Browns made the decision to sign Robert Griffin III to be their starting quarterback in 2016 and to trade out of the No. 2 pick in the draft, allowing the Eagles to draft quarterback Carson Wentz, it was clear that the Browns were focused on the future. No one outside the building thought they'd win much of anything in 2016.

They went 1–15.

At midseason 2016, the Browns traded for linebacker Jamie Collins. They had picks to spare and money to give Collins a long-term extension after the season, but Collins never became a dominant player. The Brown-DePodesta group's first pick of the 2016 Draft, wide receiver Corey Coleman, got injured early and rarely played like a starter even when he was healthy.

There were several other problems. The Brown-DePodesta group knew how to do a by-the-book teardown; their player evaluation was shaky. The Browns were stocked with draft picks and salary-cap space but were too young to win. With no quarterback

Just How Bad?

Poor drafting has probably been the biggest reason the Browns were so bad for so long. That's not a secret. But "bad" doesn't even really begin to describe how bad it was, so let's go a little further.

Despite having multiple first-round picks five times from 2012 to '18, none of those players made a Pro Bowl until Myles Garrett (2017) and Denzel Ward (2018) both did following the 2018 season. Of the Browns' 11 first-round picks from 2012 to '17, only three made it more than two seasons with the team.

The Browns from 1999 to 2015 made 20 first-round picks, and those 20 players went on to average about 43 starts with the Browns. That was the lowest number leaguewide by a wide margin.

In that same time period, just three first-round picks, three second-round picks, and four third-round picks signed second contracts with the Browns. No first-round pick got a true second contract until Joe Thomas, who was picked in 2007. Kellen Winslow Jr.'s contract was redone following the 2005 motorcycle accident that forced him to miss the entire season. It was redone with the intent of giving Winslow the chance to recoup some of the money he'd lost for violating the dangerous activities clause in his contract.

In 2013, the Browns got just 22 total starts from their five draft picks, none of whom made it past three seasons with the team. The Browns had multiple first-round picks in 2012, 2014, and 2015, and of those six players only defensive tackle Danny Shelton made it to a third season with the Browns. He was traded to the Patriots before his fourth season.

From 1999 to 2018, the Browns drafted just three players who were named first-team All-Pro. Thomas earned that honor six times. Josh Gordon, a 2012 second-round Supplemental Draft pick, was named first-team All-Pro in 2013. And 2012 second-round offensive tackle Mitchell Schwartz earned the honor in 2018, but he did it with the Chiefs.

in place, it was hard to make a case that the Browns had actually begun to build anything. With the Browns winless three months into the 2017 season, the Haslams fired Brown and replaced him with John Dorsey.

The picks and money that been hoarded made the job attractive to Dorsey. The Browns had spent $17 million to acquire an extra 2018 second-round pick from the Texans in the Brock Osweiler trade, and by passing on quarterback again in the 2017 Draft they'd added the Texans' first-round pick in a trade. Dorsey took over a team that had four of the first 35 picks in the 2018 draft and almost $100 million in cap space.

Brown had done some good things in his time running the football operation. The Browns shouldn't have taken Wentz if the Browns weren't fully ready to unify and commit to him, but taking Cody Kessler in the third round didn't make things better. The Osweiler trade made sense as part of a full rebuild; not having any real plan for quarterback heading into 2017 made no sense. The Browns got a fourth-round pick in a trade for punter Andy Lee and cleared the books and locker room of a bunch of veteran players who weren't long for the league anyway. But the Haslams were running out of patience, and after a period of historic losing the owners decided it was time to ditch patience and try to sign players good enough to return the Browns to relevance.

39 The Brothers McCown

Some were tall. Some were short. Some were highly drafted. Some were thrown into impossible situations.

Of the 30 quarterbacks to start for the new-era Browns in their first 20 seasons of existence, only two were brothers: Luke and Josh McCown.

Josh McCown came to the Browns late in a winding career that had included four different teams in his first seven NFL seasons and a detour via the Hartford Colonials of the United Football League. He signed with the Browns just before the 2015 season to both compete with and serve as babysitter for Johnny Manziel. He ended up going 1–10 as a starter in two seasons for the Browns, but in a 2015 win at Baltimore he threw for a franchise record 457 yards.

Josh McCown had already seen a little of everything by the time he arrived in Cleveland. He'd been traded, replaced, won games as an emergency backup, and flopped as a starter. He played his best football as a pro in Chicago in 2013, parlaying that into a big contract with the Buccaneers. When that didn't work, the quarterback-desperate Browns signed him just before the start of the 2015 league year.

His record-setting performance in Baltimore made McCown the first passer in franchise history to record three consecutive 300-yard games. Considering the circumstances under which McCown played with the Browns and the (old) franchise's quarterback lineage, that's some pretty impressive work.

Josh, the older brother by two years, played college football at Sam Houston State. He was a third-round pick of the Cardinals in

The Saddest Jersey Ever

Before there was this book, there was another way to track the saddest quarterback story in the history of quarterback stories.

Brokaw, Inc. is an advertising agency on West 6th Street in Cleveland, just a few blocks from Cleveland Browns Stadium. Owner Tim Brokaw had placed a Tim Couch jersey on a mannequin in a window of the agency, and later he used duct tape and a black Sharpie marker to place the name of each new quarterback who started a game for the Browns on the back of that jersey. Brokaw ended up using a lot of duct tape as the Browns cycled through quarterbacks for 17 seasons.

It's not like the mannequin was the only place for fans to track the constant change and the list that for a long time grew by two to three names each fall. But the jersey had plenty of visibility, and in the social media age pictures of it spread not only throughout Northeast Ohio, but through the country. It was free publicity for Brokaw and a sad reminder for Browns fans of their team's struggles.

On Sundays in the fall, thousands of Browns fans walk past Brokaw, Inc.—a few of them stagger—heading to or from the stadium. What started as a replica No. 2 jersey had all sorts of additions, edits, and changes through the years. By the end, it had 24 names down the right side of the back of the jersey, and nearly all the way to the ground.

After the Cleveland Cavaliers ended Cleveland's 52-year pro sports title drought by winning the NBA championship in 2016, Brokaw decided it was time to retire the jersey. What started as a harmless joke became an unintentionally popular joke, and to many it wasn't funny anymore. So the company used its social media accounts to formally announce the jersey was being retired in hopes of cutting out "bad juju" and hoping to inspire the Browns to follow the Cavaliers' lead.

"The dark cloud," the posts said, "has been lifted."

By Christmas 2018, the same mannequin in the same Brokaw, Inc., window had a new jersey.

A brown Baker Mayfield No. 6. The first jersey is dead. Apparently, hope lives.

2002. Luke was picked in the fourth round by the Browns in 2004 after starring at Louisiana Tech.

Josh McCown is remembered for his toughness and his positivity in trying times for the Browns. Luke McCown wasn't around long enough to be remembered for much of anything besides being forced to make his NFL debut against the Patriots the week after Butch Davis walked away from the Browns in the 2004 season.

In one of the most exhausting weeks in the new Browns' history, Davis resigned on a Tuesday and Terry Robiskie took over for the season's final month. The previous day, X-rays revealed that Kelly Holcomb had suffered cracked ribs during the Browns' wild loss in Cincinnati.

With Jeff Garcia still out due to a shoulder issue, that left Luke McCown, who hadn't yet played a regular season snap. The Patriots, who were on their way to winning a second straight Super Bowl title, returned the opening kickoff of that game for a touchdown, then teed off on McCown and the overmatched Browns for the rest of the afternoon.

Luke McCown started the next three games, too; the Browns lost all four. He was traded to the Buccaneers the following summer as part of a complete cleanout of the Browns' quarterback room. He ended up lasting more than a decade as a backup in Tampa Bay, Jacksonville, Atlanta, and New Orleans, playing in 62 career games and making 10 starts.

40 Lighting Money on Fire

The Browns aren't the only franchise that's made its share of regrettable big-money, big-name splashes in free agency. It tends to happen often at wide receiver, a position full of players who crave the spotlight and tend to crash hard.

The new-era Browns have struck out badly with Dwayne Bowe and Kenny Britt, players who got paid and then produced little. But both of those players were on bad Browns teams, and those decisions tend to blend in with dozens of other poor ones made at that time.

Longtime fans would say no decision was worse than the 1995 Browns making Andre Rison the highest-paid wide receiver in league history at the time. No one knew the extent of owner Art Modell's financial issues at the time, and a few months after signing Rison, Modell entered into a deal to move the team to Baltimore.

Rison's five-year contract worth a little over $17 million included a $5 million signing bonus for which Modell had to take out a personal loan.

"For the first time in my career," Rison said at the time, "I feel truly appreciated."

Rison, 28 when he signed with the Browns, had 56 touchdown catches in his first five NFL seasons with the Falcons, who decided they couldn't afford to keep him. The Packers had also been recruiting Rison but wouldn't go over $15 million on a five-year deal.

Rison would last just one season with the Browns. He caught 47 passes for 701 yards—both career-lows at the time—in 1995. From there he'd play with the Packers, Jaguars, Chiefs, and Raiders, posting just one more big season by his own high standards. With debt mounting, Modell had long been working on a behind-the-scenes deal to move the team, and in November 1995, the stunning move was announced.

Bowe's no-show cost the 2015 Browns $9 million for five catches. Bowe had signed a two-year deal before the 2015 season but played in just seven games. In 2017, the same regime that ditched Bowe signed Britt to a four-year, $32.5 million contract. Britt caught 18 passes in nine games, provided nothing in the leadership department for a young team and basically laughed his way to the bank.

Britt and first-round bust Corey Coleman were sent home from an October 2017 game in Houston for breaking curfew. Both were injured and weren't going to play the next day, and at that time it became more clear that neither was doing much to help the team. But the Browns were heavily invested in both, and not just in the cost of commercial plane tickets back to Cleveland.

In his first day on the job in December 2018, new general manager John Dorsey cut Britt, who had made $10.5 million in guaranteed money from the Browns.

41 Snapping the Streak

The Browns entered the 2018 season having lost 17 straight games. Their opener was played in bizarre weather conditions that included heavy rain and November-like temperatures on the second weekend of September. The Steelers dominated the first 45-plus minutes before the Browns defense took over, and Josh Gordon's only catch in what would become his last game with the Browns sent the game to overtime tied at 21.

It ended in a tie, too. The Steelers turned the ball over again in overtime, then blocked a field goal try by Browns kicker Zane Gonzalez. In New Orleans the next week, Gonzalez faltered again and the Saints escaped with a late victory. The Browns were 0–2 and Hue Jackson's job was likely on the line five days later when the Jets came to town for a Thursday night game.

The Jets dominated the first 20-plus minutes, and it felt like the same old Browns still played in FirstEnergy Stadium. The Jets sacked Tyrod Taylor three times in the first two quarters, and Taylor left the game due to a concussion.

Then Baker Mayfield showed up and saved the day. The stadium hadn't been that loud or wild since 2002.

The No. 1 pick in the 2018 Draft played with poise and moxie in his NFL debut despite not having taken any practice snaps with the No. 1 offense. Mayfield took over with 1:42 left in the second quarter and the Browns down 14–0. The Browns got a field goal before the half and carried the momentum over to the second half. Mayfield kept making plays as fans chanted his name.

Mayfield threw for 201 yards as the Browns won, 21–17. The Browns snapped a 19-game winless streak and won for the first time in 635 days.

Mayfield played the rest of the season, though in typical Jackson fashion he was hesitant to name the rookie the starter right after the game. The Browns went on to finish the season at 7–8–1 after Jackson and offensive coordinator Todd Haley were fired at midseason.

Mayfield set a new NFL record for most touchdown passes by a rookie with 27—19 of those coming in the eight games after the coaching change—and Freddie Kitchens was hired as head coach after calling the plays in the second half of the season.

42 Nick Chubb, Hidden Gem?

Trent Richardson was good enough as a rookie in 2012 that he bested Jim Brown's rookie season, setting new Browns rookie records with 950 rushing yards and 11 touchdowns. But the No. 3 pick never found traction after that, playing in just two games for the Browns past his rookie season and playing just two more seasons in the NFL.

Richardson's franchise rookie yardage record stood for six years until another bruising back from the SEC broke it. Nick Chubb, a second-round pick out of Georgia, finished the 2018 season with 997 yards.

Brown's 942 yards in 1957 now stand third in team history. Brown had nine rushing touchdowns that season, one ahead of the eight Chubb and Isaiah Crowell (2014) got in their respective rookie seasons. With two receiving touchdowns, Chubb's total of 10 rookie touchdowns left him tied with Brown and Eric Metcalf (1989) for the second-most by a rookie in team history.

In 2012, Richardson was able to amass those 11 touchdowns while playing on a bad offense and playing through injury. But the Browns made a regime change and a coaching change in his second season, and as he struggled to gain confidence and find rush lanes, the new front office of Joe Banner and Mike Lombardi had no choice but to accept a future first-round pick for him in what at the time was a stunning trade made just two games into the 2013 season. It would have been a brilliant trade had the Browns followed up and used that pick to acquire a key piece. Instead, another new front office regime used it on Johnny Manziel.

Ironically, Jim Brown made headlines not long after the Browns drafted Richardson when the Hall of Famer said he believed Richardson was "ordinary." It turned out Brown was right, but that didn't help the Browns. After Richardson was traded in 2013, Brown called the move "brilliant." Brown has long served in an advisory role under different regimes for the Browns and has been privy to dozens of moves that proved to be far from brilliant.

But the Browns might have hit a home run in taking Chubb at the No. 35 pick in 2018. Running back was near the top of the team's offseason priority list after Crowell was allowed to depart via

Nick Chubb runs past Erik Harris of the Raiders on his way to a touchdown during a September 2018 game in Oakland. (D. Ross Cameron/AP Photo)

free agency to the Jets. The Browns liked Penn State running back Saquon Barkley but were always taking a quarterback—and always taking Baker Mayfield, specifically—at No. 1. Barkley went to the Giants at No. 2 overall, and though the Browns also liked San Diego State running back Rashaad Penny, they turned their focus to Chubb after the Seahawks selected Penny late in the first round.

Chubb actually went over 1,000 yards for the season before losing yards in the season finale against the Ravens, one of the league's top defenses. His rookie season numbers are especially impressive because he was only the feature back for nine games, and before then-coach Hue Jackson and offensive coordinator Todd Haley were fired, general manager John Dorsey had to trade starting running back Carlos Hyde to essentially force Jackson and Haley to play Chubb. Hyde was traded to Jacksonville on a Friday afternoon, fewer than 48 hours before the Browns played and well after the week of preparation had ended.

Chubb made the most of his newfound opportunities. He had four games of at least 100 yards rushing.

The new-era Browns had generally employed older running backs on their second or third tries. The only 1,000-yard rushers since 1999 are Jamal Lewis (1,304 in 2007 and 1,002 in 2008), Reuben Droughns (1,232 in 2005), and Peyton Hillis (1,177 in 2010). All three had played for at least one other team before joining the Browns.

43 The 1,000-Yard Receiving Club

Statistics often tell only part of the story. Team decision-makers sometimes believe stats are for fans—or for agents negotiating new contracts for their players.

But numbers make good conversation pieces. They make for good bar arguments and for good book filler, too.

For the Browns, one stat stands out as strange. A team that's had three Hall of Fame pass-catchers only has had 11 players go over 1,000 receiving yards in a season. Only two have done it twice: Mac Speedie, an All-Pro end who played for the Browns from their inception in 1946 through 1952, and Hall of Fame tight end Ozzie Newsome.

Josh Gordon's 1,646 receiving yards (in 14 games) in 2013 crushed the previous record of 1,289 set by Braylon Edwards in 2007 (the year when Edwards also set the franchise record with 16 touchdown catches and Derek Anderson set the franchise record for most passing yards in a season). Gordon would go on to play just 11 more games for the Browns over the next five seasons due to multiple suspensions.

Newsome snuck over the four-digit mark twice during his impressive streak of 150 consecutive games with a reception, getting 1,002 yards in 1981 and 1,001 in 1984, the only season in which he was named first-team All-Pro. Newsome's 89-catch seasons in 1983 and '84 stood as the most catches in a single season in team history until Kellen Winslow Jr. also had 89 in 2006, his first full season after breaking his leg as a rookie then nearly dying after a motorcycle accident in 2005. Winslow's lone 1,000-yard season came in 2007, when he had 1,106 yards on 82 catches.

The top season in terms of receiving yards in the old Browns era was 1,236 by Webster Slaughter in 1989, when Slaughter averaged an impressive 19 yards per reception. Slaughter was a two-time Pro Bowler in his 12-year career and was an important piece of the Browns' offense from 1986 to 1991.

That players like Speedie and Hall of Famer Paul Warfield played 12 or 14-game schedules—and not in a pass-happy era—makes their numbers that much more impressive. Speedie averaged 16.1 yards per reception for his career and twice led the AAFL in receiving yards per game. He had 1,146 receiving yards in 1947 and 1,028 in 1949; he led the league in both years. In his final year, 1952, he led the NFL with 62 receptions in 12 games. Hall of Famer Dante Lavelli was the go-to receiver for many of those early Browns teams, but Speedie was the big-play guy.

Warfield got 1,067 yards on just 50 catches in 1968, when he also led the NFL with 12 touchdown catches on a 14-game schedule. Other Browns pass-catchers to go over 1,000 yards in a season are Kevin Johnson (1,097 in 2001), tight end Gary Barnidge (1,043 in 2015), Antonio Bryant (1,009 in 2005), and Terrelle Pryor (1,007 in 2016).

44 Kessler and Kizer

When the Browns passed on the chance to take Carson Wentz in the 2016 Draft and drafted Cody Kessler in the third round, then-coach Hue Jackson tried to take one for the team's analytics-driven front office.

"Trust me on this one," Jackson said.

It worked as well as most of Jackson's other proclamations in his 2.5 years as coach. Kessler had few traits of an NFL starting quarterback. He was not exceptional in any one area and really had no business either being picked in the third round or being on an NFL field. But when the Browns lost Robert Griffin III to injury in the first game of 2016 and Josh McCown got hurt in the second game, Kessler had to play.

The Browns actually should have won Kessler's first game as the starter. They led the Dolphins at halftime and rallied from 11 down in the fourth quarter, but fill-in kicker Cody Parkey missed a 46-yard field goal on the final play of regulation and the Dolphins won in overtime.

The Browns drafted DeShone Kizer in the second round in 2017. They liked Kizer's arm strength. He had left Notre Dame with two years of eligiblity remaining and hadn't exactly been great in his final college season, but Kizer looked like an NFL quarterback and had some upside.

The problem is the Browns had no real plan at quarterback in 2017. Griffin and McCown were gone. After going 0–8 as a rookie starter, Kessler piloted the starters through the spring and opened training camp as the starter, but he faded quickly. The Browns had essentially paid $17 million for a second-round pick from the Texans but also had acquired Brock Osweiler. Instead of dumping Osweiler after the trade, the Browns kept him around. Kessler started the first preseason game, Osweiler started the second, and by the time Kizer went 6-of-18 as the starter in the third, it was clear he was the best option even though he wasn't ready. In the regular season, Kizer threw 11 touchdowns and 22 interceptions and was sacked 38 times.

The Browns sat Kizer for one game, making Kevin Hogan the 28th player in the new era to start a game at quarterback. That game in Houston was a disaster. Kizer was back in the lineup the next week, and the Browns were positioning themselves for the No. 1 pick by Halloween.

That part worked. Top personnel exec Sashi Brown didn't survive the season; he was replaced in December 2017 by John Dorsey. In his first offseason as general manager, Dorsey traded Kizer, Kessler, and Hogan. The Browns traded for Tyrod Taylor, drafted Baker Mayfield with that No. 1 pick, and went forward believing that the number of starting quarterbacks in the new era for a long time would sit on No. 30 with Mayfield, who replaced Taylor in the first month of the 2018 season.

45 Trading Down

The Browns drafted Clay Matthews, a linebacker out of USC, in the first round in 1978. They did not draft Clay Matthews III, a linebacker out of USC, in the first round in 2009.

In fact, for a while it looked as though the Browns wouldn't draft *anyone* in the first round of the 2009 Draft. Coach Eric Mangini and GM George Kokinis wanted more players, more picks, and in a plan that felt very much like an impression of the Patriot Way, the Browns began trading down.

First, the Browns traded out of the fifth spot in the draft, where they were originally scheduled to pick, in a trade with the Jets at 17. From there they traded back with the Buccaneers at 19, and then with the Eagles at 21, where they finally made a pick, taking Cal center Alex Mack.

Mack turned out to be a rare first-round success story for the new-era Browns. He was a reliable player and a three-time Pro

Bowler for the Browns, but the Browns never found a quarterback or a dominant pass-rusher during that time.

Mack wasn't the issue. It was the rest of the 2009 Draft that turned out to be so disappointing—and put the Browns at a disadvantage going forward. Second-round wide receivers Brian Robiskie and Mohammed Massaquoi never became more than average, and second-round linebacker David Veikune lasted just one season with the Browns. Kamerion Wimbley's production had dropped off greatly past his rookie year, leaving the Browns with a major need.

Fourth-round linebacker Kaluka Maiava had a decent career as a backup and a special teams player, and sixth-round safety Don Carey had a similar but longer career—just not for the Browns. The Browns placed him on the waived-injured list during his training camp to create an open roster spot, and the Jaguars claimed Carey via waivers. In part due to Mangini's infatuation with the bottom of the roster, the Browns took an unnecessary risk and lost Carey for it.

Sixth-round defensive back Coye Francies never did much with the Browns, and though sixth-round running back James Davis showed some flashes, he ended up getting injured during practice and was gone by his second season. He ended up playing nine career games with the Browns and Redskins, averaging 2.7 yards per carry.

In those draft-day trades, Mangini got a bunch of late-round picks and a bunch of mid-level players from the Jets such as Kenyon Coleman and Abe Elam. Mangini knew they'd add smarts and experience to the locker room, but the Browns needed talent. The 2009 team started 1–11 as the Browns had typical quarterback issues and faded late in games.

By midseason, general manager Kokinis was gone. Without public explanation, he was escorted out of the building on a

Monday morning, the day after an embarrassing loss in Chicago. After the season, owner Randy Lerner stripped Mangini of his personnel powers and hired Mike Holmgren as team president.

46 A Memorable Loss in New England

The Browns' nearly unexplainable loss in New England on December 8, 2013, is memorable for a few reasons.

It was the beginning of the end for coach Rob Chudzinski. The Browns led 19–3 late in the third quarter and 26–14 with 2:39 left, but lost the game, 27–26, after failing to recover an onside kick. It was the fourth straight loss for the Browns, who lost their final seven games. Chudzinski became the only full-time coach in team history to last just one season.

It was the fourth straight big game for wide receiver Josh Gordon, who was in his second season at the time. Though it wasn't Gordon's best game of that season by the numbers, he dominated smaller defensive backs in the pass game and ran by them after the catch. He caught seven passes for 151 yards and also led the Browns with 34 rushing yards gained on a reverse.

Gordon's 774 receiving yards over a four-game stretch concluding with that game were an NFL record. He scored an 80-yard touchdown on a slant from Jason Campbell, catching the ball and sprinting away from cornerback Aqib Talib. The previous week, he'd scored a 95-yard touchdown.

The Browns thought they'd found a star. Gordon led the NFL in receiving in 2013 in just 14 games; he'd missed the first two due to suspension. He'd only play 11 more games for the Browns over the following five seasons before being traded to the Patriots two weeks into the 2018 season.

Bill Belichick doesn't forget much, and five years later when he traded for Gordon it's fair to assume Belichick remembered that day.

The Browns had gone up 19–3 on Gordon's touchdown with 1:25 left in the third quarter. The Patriots immediately answered to make it 19–11, then cut it to 19–14 with 5:43 left on a 50-yard field goal. But Gordon's 34-yard reverse came on the ensuing drive, and he then caught a 19-yard pass to put the Browns in scoring position. They extended the lead to 12 on a short touchdown pass from Campbell to tight end Jordan Cameron, who also went to the Pro Bowl that season.

The Patriots cut the deficit to one score on a short touchdown pass from Tom Brady to Julian Edelman with 1:04 left, and an unnecessary roughness call on Browns safety Jordan Poyer after the play moved the onside kick attempt up 15 yards. You could also feel what happened next coming as Browns running back Fozzy Whittaker failed to recover the onside kick. The Patriots got the ball, got a big pass interference call on rookie Browns cornerback Leon McFadden, and scored with 35 seconds left to take the lead.

The Browns got the ball to the Patriots' 40-yard line in the final seconds, but Billy Cundiff's 58-yard field goal at the buzzer never had much of a chance.

47 Calling on Colt

Colt McCoy was a successful college quarterback who handled the spotlight and pressures that come with holding one of the highest-profile jobs in the state of Texas.

In the NFL, he had average size, average arm strength, and not much chance to save any organization. In the third round in 2010, the Browns took him anyway.

The Browns were two years away from not having a shot at Andrew Luck and not trading up for Robert Griffin III, instead settling on using a first-round pick on Brandon Weeden. McCoy entered a quarterback room that already had Jake Delhomme and Seneca Wallace, both veteran backup types who brought leadership and savvy but weren't going to be the team's long-awaited answer.

The Browns started that 2010 Draft, Tom Heckert's first as general manager, with solid picks in cornerback Joe Haden and safety T.J. Ward. In the third round, team president Mike Holmgren later admitted to "pulling rank" in the draft room and dictating the McCoy pick. That was another piece of evidence that Holmgren either should have been coaching the Browns himself or shouldn't have been involved at all. The Browns were paying Holmgren big money to be a part-time figurehead and part-time picker of mediocre quarterbacks.

In 2014, Holmgren admitted he should have coached the Browns. At that point, he was four years too late. Holmgren said then-owner Randy Lerner didn't want him to be the coach, and Holmgren believed since he was unsure of his desire to coach again, it was best that he focus on his executive role.

McCoy had some decent moments with the Browns; considering the low bar, his positive touchdown to interception ratio of

14-to-11 in 2011 was progress for the team. But in December of that season, McCoy took a cheap shot from Steelers linebacker James Harrison and suffered a concussion. The Browns allowed McCoy to go back in the game not long after, setting off a public war of words between McCoy's father, Brad, and then-coach Pat Shurmur.

After the game, McCoy was diagnosed with a concussion and missed the rest of the season.

McCoy went 6–15 as a starter with the Browns in 2010–11. He served as Brandon Weeden's backup in 2012, then was traded to the 49ers ahead of the 2013 season. After one season there, McCoy found a home with the Washington Redskins as their primary backup and headed to the 2019 season in line to at least be the team's temporary starter.

48 Dorsey Moves Fast

When he took over the football operation in December 2017, new general manager John Dorsey had two primary advantages on his predecessors.

One was the treasure trove of draft picks and cap space that the Sashi Brown-led Browns had acquired. That was probably the top recruiting tool owner Jimmy Haslam had in his pursuit of Dorsey, who'd been fired by the Chiefs in the summer of 2017 but had spent the fall scouting college prospects.

The other was time. Getting hired in early December meant Dorsey would get four in-season weeks in the building to begin his work and evaluations. Most general managers are hired in January, when the current players are gone and the entire building is in a transition phase.

In his first game, three days after he was hired, the Browns should have beaten the Green Bay Packers. It took an epic collapse in the fourth quarter against a depleted Packers team to keep the nightmare of 0–16 alive. But Dorsey had three more games—and three more practice weeks—to observe and get to know players in the locker room.

Before free agency officially started in March, he made four trades. DeShone Kizer was gone, shipped to Green Bay after 15 starts where he'd become a backup like he should have been with the Browns. The Browns gave up Kizer and swapped some mid-round picks with the Packers in return for Damarious Randall, a cornerback who would return to his more natural position at safety.

The Browns also acquired Tyrod Taylor from the Bills. Taylor would serve as the team's transitional quarterback as Dorsey had planned all along to take a quarterback at No. 1 in the 2018 Draft. Arguably the league's worst receiving corps then got a boost when the Browns traded with the Dolphins to acquire Jarvis Landry, who through four seasons had caught more passes than any player in his first four seasons in NFL history. Landry had worn out his welcome in Miami, though, and the Browns were willing to give him the kind of rich contract the Dolphins weren't.

Dorsey also traded nose tackle Danny Shelton, a 2015 first-round pick, to the Patriots. Later that summer he'd also ship off 2016 first-round pick Corey Coleman. Few jobs were safe, and they shouldn't have been. Dorsey was hired to clean up the mess and make the Browns competitive; they needed to get older and get better, and it's almost always the high picks or the priority free agents of the past regime who are first to go.

Taylor only ended up starting three games before Baker Mayfield took his job. Randall had a great year at his more natural free safety spot, and Landry led the 2018 Browns with 81 receptions.

By the time the rosters were trimmed to the regular-season size of 53 on Labor Day Weekend, the Browns had a staggering 31 players who weren't on the previous year's active roster. Even for an organization that had constantly been in flux, that was significant turnover.

John Dorsey answers questions a week before the 2018 Draft during a news conference at Browns' headquarters in Berea, Ohio. (Tony Dejak/AP Photo)

49 The 0-fer Club

From 2008 to 2016, the Browns had at least three different starting quarterbacks in six different seasons. Only once in the first 20 years of the new era did one quarterback start all 16 games, Tim Couch in 2001. Only four quarterbacks started on opening day more than once, and none did it more than twice.

Those four are Couch, Kelly Holcomb, Charlie Frye, and Brandon Weeden.

There's another, more dubious club that explains the struggles of the new-era Browns. Among the 30 who started a game in the first 20 seasons back, 16 of them made at least one start in a given season without getting a win.

The lead dog here—if you can call it that—is DeShone Kizer, who made 15 starts in the 0–16 season in 2017. The Browns rushed the second-round rookie into duty with a bad team, giving him little chance to win. John Dorsey did Kizer a favor when he traded him to the Packers ahead of Kizer's second season, making Kizer a backup and giving him a chance to learn and recover.

Cody Kessler went 0–8 as a rookie starter in 2016. He was overmatched and overwhelmed in a season that saw the Browns lose their first two quarterbacks in the first two weeks and have to play six different players at quarterback over the course of that season.

Going 0–1 were Spergon Wynn in 2000, Charlie Frye in 2007, Bruce Gradkowski in 2008, Thaddeus Lewis in 2012, Connor Shaw in 2014, and Kevin Hogan in 2017. Frye started the opener, got benched, and got traded the next day. Wynn's claim to fame was that the Browns drafted him a few spots ahead of where the Patriots got some guy named Tom Brady.

Ty Detmer was 0–2 in 1999. Luke McCown was 0–4 in 2004. Derek Anderson was 0–3 in 2006 before getting hot and going to the Pro Bowl in 2007. Weeden was 0–5 in 2013. He was benched and released before the next season.

50 Best Drafts

The new-era Browns produced plenty of candidates for the title of worst draft class in franchise history. That so many of them were stacked together led to the Browns going more than a decade without a winning season and setting NFL records for futility by going 4–44 from 2015 to '17.

But what was the best draft class in team history? There are really three choices.

The Browns took running back Jim Brown with pick No. 6 in the 1957 Draft. In the second round they selected quarterback Milt Plum, and in the seventh round they selected guard Gene Hickerson, who later joined Brown in the Hall of Fame. The Browns picked another Hall of Famer in the fifth round in defensive tackle Henry Jordan, but he played just two seasons as a backup for the Browns before finding stardom with the Packers.

In 1964, Hall of Fame wide receiver Paul Warfield was picked in the first round and Hall of Fame running back Leroy Kelly was picked in the eighth round.

In 1978, linebacker Clay Matthews and tight end Ozzie Newsome were both picked in the first round. Matthews and Newsome combined to play in a staggering 476 games over the course of their respective careers. Newsome is in the Hall of Fame after catching passes in 150 consecutive games, and he remains the franchise receiving leader. Matthews has been a Hall of Fame finalist. He's the Browns' all-time leader with 62 sacks and 232 games played.

The 1972 Draft makes the list. It started with safety Thom Darden, the franchise's all-time interceptions leader, and included a nice find in the 13th round in quarterback Brian Sipe, who went on to set several franchise passing records.

In the new era, the 2018 Draft stands out as a potential franchise changer given that No. 1 overall pick Baker Mayfield set the NFL rookie record for touchdown passes and No. 4 pick Denzel Ward went to the Pro Bowl as a rookie. Second-round running back Nick Chubb set the franchise rookie rushing record, but it's dangerous to jump to any conclusions—good or bad—after one season.

The 2006 class was far from outstanding, but it was far better than most in the new era. First-round linebacker Kamerion Wimbley had 11 sacks as a rookie. Second-round inside linebacker D'Qwell Jackson was a longtime starter, and fifth-round running back Jerome Harrison set the franchise record with a 286-yard rushing game in 2009. For a number of years, sixth-round fullback Lawrence Vickers was among the league's best at his position.

The 2007 Draft started with Joe Thomas, a future Hall of Famer and the best player of the new era. But the Browns traded back into the first-round and ultimately missed with quarterback Brady Quinn. Second-round cornerback Eric Wright and fifth-round cornerback Brandon McDonald became multi-year contributors.

For as bad as the first-round selections of Justin Gilbert and Johnny Manziel were in 2014, the Browns got guard Joel Bitonio in the second round and linebacker Christian Kirksey in the third. Both became team leaders and multi-year starters. The 2017 Draft started with Myles Garrett at No. 1 and included two more first-round picks, safety Jabrill Peppers and tight end David Njoku. Peppers was traded after his second season to the Giants as the Browns acquired Pro Bowl wide receiver Odell Beckham Jr. In the third round in 2017, the Browns drafted defensive tackle Larry Ogunjobi, who was disruptive in his first two years and played like a potential future star.

51 Jamir Miller's One Big Season

Jamir Miller was the first player in the Browns' new era to be named to the Pro Bowl.

He was probably the new franchise's first big hit in free agency, too. But Miller's success was short-lived. After an All-Pro season in 2001, Miller suffered a torn Achilles tendon in the 2002 preseason opener and never played again.

Miller recorded 13 sacks in 2001, the Browns' first season under defensive-minded head coach Butch Davis. That Browns team took a leap on both sides of the ball as compared to previous overmatched editions, and going forward the Browns envisioned building something nasty, with Miller and Courtney Brown rushing from the edges with Gerard Warren and Orpheus Roye leading a strong interior group. Like so many other plans in the new era, it didn't work out, as Miller never got to build on his big season and Brown never played a full season past his rookie year.

At the time, Miller's 13-sack 2001 season stood as the second-best in team history behind Reggie Camp's 14 in 1984. Miller was named first-team All-Pro after recording the highest sack total for a Browns player since Michael Dean Perry's 11.5 in 1990. Myles Garrett, the No. 1 overall pick in the 2017 Draft, bumped Miller

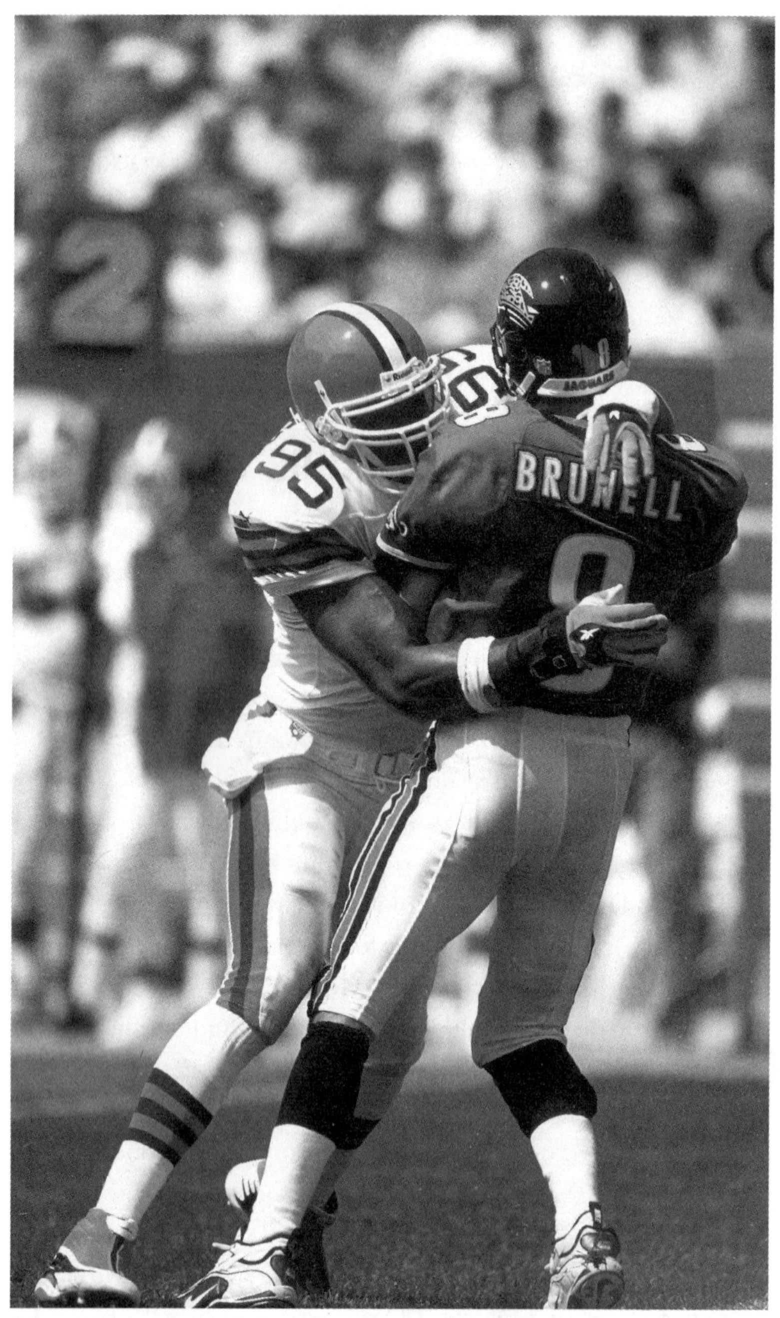

Jamir Miller sacks Mark Brunell in a September 2000 game. (Jonathan Daniel/Allsport/Getty Images)

back to third on the franchise's single-season sack list when Garrett recorded 13.5 sacks during his second season.

Miller entered the league with high expectations. He was a rangy, athletic linebacker with enough cover and rush ability that the Cardinals selected him at No. 10 overall in the 1994 NFL Draft, but he was suspended for marijuana usage early in his career and only totaled 13.5 sacks in five years in Arizona. After having just three sacks in 1998, the Cardinals were willing to let Miller test free agency. The Browns got him on a one-year deal for $1.3 million.

Midway through that 1999 season, the Browns signed Miller to a four-year extension worth about $18 million, starting with a $6 million signing bonus. At the time, that was elite pass-rusher money. But it also included a $14 million roster bonus at the beginning of the last year of the contract, 2003, so it's likely Miller wouldn't have been back with the Browns even if he hadn't been injured in 2002. Miller and his agent, Leigh Steinberg, had pushed the Browns for a new, richer deal ahead of the 2002 season, and Miller sat out some of the offseason program as a negotiating tactic. It didn't work, and Davis believed Miller's injury was at least partially tied to Miller not reporting for camp in top shape.

Citing advice from doctors and "a very discouraging medical report," per Steinberg, Miller officially retired in May 2003 at 29 years old. The Browns had pulled a one-year contract offer shortly before the announcement.

He finished his eight-year career with 36 sacks, five fumble recoveries, and two interceptions.

52 In the Trenches

For parts of two seasons, the Browns had the makings of a top-shelf offensive line. Left tackle Joe Thomas never missed a snap or a Pro Bowl. Alex Mack was one of the NFL's most consistent and athletic centers; he lived for the chance to get downfield and lay blocks on smaller defenders, many of whom couldn't believe Mack was athletic enough to catch them.

In the second round of 2014, the Browns believed college tackle Joel Bitonio would make a smooth transition to guard while playing between Mack and Thomas. It was some of their best thinking in years. Bitonio benefited from their tutoring and was athletic enough to be an instant impact player.

Mack got injured five games into the 2014 season and departed via free agency after 2015. Bitonio dealt with injuries himself in 2015 and 2016 before returning and playing up to the level of the big contract he signed before the 2017 season. When Thomas retired after that season, Bitonio became the team's longest-tenured player and the veteran leader of the offensive line.

After multiple trade-downs in the first round of Eric Mangini's only draft running the show in 2009, the Browns took Mack and were right in their assessment that he'd be a longtime staple at center. Mack was athletic, smart, and tough. He was everything the Browns hoped he'd be; various regimes just never found the right quarterback to pair with their Pro Bowl–quality center.

In seven seasons with the Browns, Mack played for four different head coaches and five different offensive coordinators. The Browns had a different opening day starting quarterback in six of those seven seasons.

The offensive line was clicking and the run game was rolling early in the 2014 season before Mack suffered a broken leg during a game against the Steelers. The Browns started 7–4 that season before faltering and finishing at 7–9; the offense was never the same with Mack sidelined for the first time in his career.

Because he played on so many bad teams and because he played in the trenches, Mack never got much attention outside the Browns' building. But he wasn't just a good player by Browns' standards; he was named to three Pro Bowls in his time with the Browns and got the same honor in each of his first three years with the Falcons. Through 10 NFL seasons, the only games he'd missed were those in 2014 after he suffered the injury. He played with a broken leg in Super Bowl LI.

Bitonio went to his first Pro Bowl following the 2018 season. A team captain and back-to-back winner of the Good Guy Award presented by the local chapter of the Pro Football Writers Association, Bitonio has long been respected in and out of the Browns' building.

53 Local Punter Makes History

Prior to 1994, the NFL did not allow teams to attempt two-point conversions after touchdowns. In the 1994 season opener vs. the Bengals, the Browns ran a fake off an extra-point attempt, and punter/holder Tom Tupa scored the first two-point conversion in NFL history.

The run earned Tupa the nickname "Two-Point Tupa." Long before he got that cheesy nickname, Tupa was a two-position player whose signing with the Browns made for a nice homecoming story.

Tupa grew up just south of Cleveland and starred at Brecksville High School before playing quarterback and punting at Ohio State. He was the Buckeyes' starting quarterback in 1987, his senior season, when he was also a consensus All-American punter. He was drafted by the Cardinals in the third round, at No. 68 overall, in 1988. In 1991, he started 11 games at quarterback for the Cardinals. He was mostly used as a punter after that in a career that also included stints with the Colts, Patriots, Jets, Buccaneers, and Redskins before Tupa retired following the 2004 season.

The Browns later had another local punter. Dave Zastudil was a multi-sport star at Bay High School, just west of Cleveland, and then played at Ohio University. The Ravens drafted Zastudil in the fourth round in 2002, and after four years there he signed with the Browns in 2006. Zastudil was the punter for some of the best special teams units in Browns' history, playing alongside kicker Phil Dawson, return specialist Joshua Cribbs, and Pro Bowl long snapper Ryan Pontbriand. The 2007 offense was so good that Zastudil only punted 49 times all season.

A 2009 injury cut his time with the Browns short, and Zastudil would miss more than a full season before catching on with the Cardinals in 2011. He punted for the Cardinals for three full seasons and part of 2014 before retiring.

The best punter in team history might be Chris Gardocki, who was not only reliable—and too busy—for the 1999–2003 Browns, but endeared himself to fans when he twice gave the middle finger to the Steelers' sideline and coach Bill Cowher during a game in 2000. Gardocki, who was upset about what he felt was a cheap shot by Joey Porter, was fined $5,000.

An All-Pro with the Colts in 1996, Gardocki led the league in punts with the Browns in 2000 and 2001. In 1999 and 2000, the local chapter of the Pro Football Writers Association named him team MVP. He retired in 2006 having posted an NFL record of

1,177 punts without having one blocked, and he averaged 43.4 yards per punt in his five seasons with the Browns.

Through 20 seasons of the new era, the Browns' career leaders in yards per punt were both still active players. Andy Lee averaged 46.7 yards per punt, but he's best known for getting traded the following season for a fourth-round pick by then-GM Sashi Brown, who made a bunch of trades in his 23 months on the job and few were better than getting a punter for a fourth-rounder. Through three seasons (2016–18) with the Browns, Britton Colquitt was averaging 46.1 yards per punt and had been one of the league's best punters during that time.

54 Mistakes Added Up

In 2010, Brady Quinn and Kamerion Wimbley were traded on the same day, Quinn to the Broncos and Wimbley to the Raiders. At the time, neither trade was exactly a front-page story, which was a problem in its own right.

By then, bad drafting had taken a painful toll on the Browns. First-round misses had compounded. Impatience had hurt all aspects of the organization, and quarterback misses had cost multiple people their jobs. Besides hitting on Joe Thomas in 2007, the first decade of drafting was a disaster.

Quinn was a much-decorated college quarterback, and the Browns gave their 2008 first-round pick to get back into the 2007 first round and get him. But he never became the team's full-time starter and lasted just three seasons. Wimbley had double-digit sacks as a rookie in 2006 but faded after that.

Neither of the new franchise's first two No.1 overall picks, Tim Couch and Courtney Brown, made it past 2004. The No. 3 overall pick of 2001, Gerard Warren, was out the door the same year Brown was. First-round pick William Green was a hero as a rookie in 2002, pushing the Browns to the playoffs. But Green only made it to 2005, two years after getting suspended by the league then getting stabbed by his girlfriend in a domestic dispute gone public.

Jeff Faine was a solid first-round pick in 2003, but he was a center. And he only made it three years before the Browns traded him to give the center job to LeCharles Bentley, who got hurt on the first play of training camp in 2006 and never played a down with the Browns after signing a $35 million contract.

The Browns needed a franchise quarterback in 2004, but they passed on Ben Roethlisberger for Kellen Winslow, who broke his leg on the field in his first year and wrecked his knee on a motorcycle the following spring. Braylon Edwards and Winslow had their moments, and each had their best season in 2007 when the Browns went 10–6 and flirted with the playoffs. But both were gone two years later, and neither reached his full potential.

It says a lot about the first decade that the quarterback of the 2007 team, Derek Anderson, was claimed via waivers. The first draft pick of the new era to make it to a second contract with the team was cornerback Daylon McCutcheon, a 1999 third-round pick who was a solid pro and a valuable player but was far from a star.

55 The AFC North

The Browns returned to the NFL in 1999 after three seasons away with their colors, their team name, and just about everything else intact. They returned to the AFC Central Division, too, offering the awkward but exciting opportunity for the new Browns to establish an on-field rivalry with the old Browns, the Baltimore Ravens.

Change was the theme of that AFC Central. The Browns became the Ravens. The Houston Oilers became the Tennessee Oilers in 1997, then the Tennessee Titans in 1999. The Jacksonville Jaguars, not central to much of anything, were placed in the AFC Central when they entered the league in 1995. They swept the Browns that year en route to finishing 4–12.

The Browns' rushed return to the league gave the NFL 31 teams, which was clearly less than ideal for scheduling purposes. Those 1999 and 2000 Browns teams had to play 16 consecutive games and had a Week 17 bye as the NFL sorted through awkward scheduling issues and figured, correctly, that the Browns wouldn't be pushing for a playoff spot. When the Houston Texans entered the league in 2002, the NFL had a much more manageable 32 teams and re-aligned, scrapping its three-division format for four divisions in each conference. And the AFC North was born.

The Browns had longtime natural rivals in the Pittsburgh Steelers and the Cincinnati Bengals. Paul Brown was a co-founder of both Ohio franchises, and the Browns-Steelers rivalry dates back to 1950. Those three were easy choices for the AFC's midwestern-based division. Buffalo also made sense based on proximity, while Indianapolis is a little over 100 miles from Cincinnati and an easy, all-highway drive from both Cleveland and Pittsburgh. But the

NFL ultimately chose the Ravens over the Bills to complete the AFC North.

At the time, the Browns and Ravens didn't have much of an on-field rivalry. The Ravens were rolling and won the Super Bowl in 2000, much to the chagrin of long-suffering Browns fans. But the Browns getting their first season sweep of the Ravens in 2007 had meaning in Cleveland, and in the years that followed, the likes of Phil Savage and Jamal Lewis joining the Browns gave that rivalry some extra juice. Ravens-Steelers grew into one of the NFL's most physical and competitive rivalries over those same years, and after years of misery, the Bengals occasionally popped up with a team good enough to contend for the division crown.

In the new divisional alignment, the Jaguars went to the AFC South along with the Texans, Colts, and the Titans. The Bills stayed in the AFC East to protect their in-state rivalry with the Jets and their longstanding rivalries with the Patriots and Dolphins. The Colts probably made for a more complicated decision as the Dolphins clearly made the better geographic fit for the AFC South, but history and rivalries won out in keeping the Dolphins in the AFC East. The four AFC East teams had been in the same division since the 1960s.

In 2002, the Browns went 6–2 on the road and used a big December to make the playoffs, but they never really threatened the Steelers atop the division. The Steelers finished 10–5–1; the Browns were 9–7. The Browns' strongest run at an AFC North title came in 2007, when they lost a tiebreaker to the Steelers based on getting swept in the season series. Had Willie McGinest not let Ben Roethlisberger escape from his grasp on a fourth-quarter touchdown drive, the Browns might have won the division in 2007 and a lot might be different. Alas, Roethlisberger and the Steelers kept rolling and the Browns kept losing and changing.

On the 15th anniversary of the first round of the 2004 Draft, Roethlisberger signed a three-year contract extension with the

Steelers. That miss was Butch Davis' lasting legacy with the Browns.

Through 20 seasons, the new Browns were 10–30 against the old Browns. The Ravens drafted quarterback Joe Flacco in 2008, and Flacco did not lose a game to the Browns until 2013. The Browns then defeated the Ravens again in 2015 in Baltimore as Josh McCown set a franchise passing record with 457 passing yards as the Browns won in overtime. Flacco lost his last game vs. the Browns in overtime in 2018 as Baker Mayfield engineered a long drive to set up the winning field goal. Flacco got hurt and replaced later that season, and in early 2019 he was traded to the Broncos.

In 2018, the Browns escaped the AFC North basement for the first time since 2010. They swept the Bengals in 2018 for the first time since 2002.

56 The Undefeated Quarterback

Like Cody Kessler, Osweiler never won a game for the Browns. He never lost one either.

Without meeting him or having him into their building, the Texans were desperate enough to sign Osweiler to a four-year, $72 million contract. That the Broncos were hesitant to go that high should have been a red flag, but the Texans had a playoff-quality defense and believed competent quarterback play would help them play deep into January.

The rebuilding Browns essentially buying a second-round pick was a savvy move. It's fair to say Sashi Brown's strategy of trying to essentially give the Browns five drafts in three years was only going to eventually pay off had the Browns drafted good players with those picks, but at the time the Browns knew they were years from contention and weren't going to fix any of their significant issues with $16 million in 2017.

Like many things in Brown's two years running the team, the numbers made sense but the football plan—or lack thereof—for Osweiler was puzzling. The Browns debated cutting him immediately, and in retrospect they probably should have. Instead they brought Osweiler into the team's offseason program as a backup with no intention of really playing him. Perhaps they thought another trade for future draft pick would surface eventually, but none did.

Kessler was demoted about a week into training camp in 2017, and Osweiler was promoted to starter. But he fizzled quickly, too, and rookie DeShone Kizer was named the starter before the team's third preseason game, which is generally the most important of the four. The 0–16 writing was on the wall.

Osweiler was held out of the final two preseason games, and after no trade partner surfaced, the Browns decided to cut him ahead of the league-wide cut to 53-man rosters. Because his contract was guaranteed and included offset language, the Browns paid all of the $16 million Osweiler was owed minus the approximately $775,000 Osweiler made when he ended up returning to Denver on a veteran minimum contract. He made four starts for the Broncos in 2017, losing all four.

The Browns' Osweiler trade offered the Texans a much-needed financial bailout. A talented defense headlined by linemen J.J. Watt and Jadeveon Clowney needed to be fortified, and regardless of who the quarterback was, the Texans needed more offensive playmakers to try to take the burden off of Pro Bowl wide receiver DeAndre Hopkins. But the Texans had salary cap problems, and those problems were magnified by Osweiler's struggles. The Texans had given Osweiler $37 million in guarantees and paid him $21 million in that first year.

Six weeks later, the Browns and Texans traded again, with the Browns offering the Texans a second quarterback bailout. The Browns agreed to move out of the No. 12 slot in the 2017 Draft, passing on a quarterback again and allowing the Texans to select Deshaun Watson of Clemson. The price for the Texans to move up 13 slots included the Texans' 2018 first-round pick. The Browns took the future pick, selected safety Jabrill Peppers with what had been the Texans' pick at No. 25 and addressed quarterback in the second round with Kizer, an Ohio native.

Watson got off to a strong start in his rookie season. He dissected the overmatched Browns in an October game in Houston, one in which the Browns benched Kizer and went with Kevin Hogan as their starting quarterback. But after Watson suffered a torn ACL a few weeks later, the Texans' 2017 season went in the tank and the Browns ended up with the No. 4 overall pick in 2018. They used that on cornerback Denzel Ward, who went to the Pro Bowl as a rookie. They used the Osweiler pick at No. 35 on running back Nick Chubb, who set the Browns' rookie rushing record.

57 Passing on Julio

One good thing about the 2011 Draft for the Browns is they didn't get suckered into taking quarterbacks Jake Locker, Blaine Gabbert, or Christian Ponder, all of whom went in the top 12 and never came close to playing to their draft position.

And that's about where the good news ends.

The Browns, sitting at No. 6, couldn't get quarterback Cam Newton or pass-rusher Von Miller. They really liked Georgia wide receiver A.J. Green, but Green went to the Bengals at No. 4. The Browns could have stayed at No. 6 and picked Alabama wide receiver Julio Jones, who was big and fast and immediately would have been the most talented wide receiver on the Browns' roster by a wide margin.

The Browns passed. They traded out. The Falcons traded up, and Jones went on to have a Hall of Fame type of career in Atlanta. The Browns got five picks over two seasons for one pick, but as was the story of other draft-day trades, they never cashed them in.

After initially dropping to pick No. 27 in the trade, the Browns ended up trading two of the picks they received from the Falcons to move up to No. 21 and select defensive tackle Phil Taylor. They later turned those extra picks into wide receiver Greg Little, full-back Owen Marecic, and quarterback Brandon Weeden in the first round in 2012.

Flop, flop, and flop. Even if the Haslam Family hadn't purchased the Browns in 2012 and begun a cycle of constantly cleaning out the front office, general manager Tom Heckert would have been fired after 2012. Trading the rights to Jones for a defensive tackle and a bunch of average guys wasn't helping the Browns recover from what was becoming a long stint of losing.

A decent run-stopper in his years with the Browns, Taylor never became anything close to a star. Taylor made 42 starts in parts of four seasons with the Browns but was never fully healthy past his rookie season. The Browns cut Taylor in training camp in 2015 despite his $5 million salary for that season being guaranteed. A knee injury left him unable to play in 2015, and though the Broncos gave him a shot the following season, he ultimately landed on the injured reserve list. He later had stints with the Bucs and Redskins, but never again played in a real game due to injury.

58 Oh, Romeo

Romeo Crennel's first stint with the Browns didn't go well. But it led to Crennel catching on with the Patriots, where he won three Super Bowls in four seasons as defensive coordinator before being hired by the Browns in 2005.

Crennel's first shot to be a defensive coordinator came with the Browns in 2000 but lasted just one season, as Chris Palmer's entire staff was fired at the end of the year. Crennel had come from the Bill Parcells coaching tree, and in his previous job coaching defensive linemen with the Jets and Giants he established a relationship with Bill Belichick, who hired Crennel as his defensive coordinator in 2001.

Three Super Bowl rings later, Crennel was Phil Savage's pick to become head coach of the Browns in 2005. But the Browns did not get the next Belichick. Crennel coached the Browns to their only 10-win season of the new era in 2007, but he was fired after the Browns went 4–12 the next year.

Crennel had a grandfatherly presence, causing some to believe he was too nice. He had to fire his first choice for offensive coordinator, Maurice Carthon, in 2006, as the Browns couldn't generate much of anything offensively. He never built a dominant defense in Cleveland. With the exception of Derek Anderson's three red-hot months in 2007, the Browns never generated enough offense. Crennel had the respect of the locker room and of the organization as a whole, but he never had a top quarterback or a dominant pass-rusher on his Browns teams.

During the Anderson–Charlie Frye quarterback competition in 2007 training camp, Crennel said it was so close that he flipped a coin to decide that Frye would get to start the preseason opener.

All In

The 2008 Draft was a Browns draft unlike any other. Phil Savage had traded the team's first-round pick away during the 2007 Draft, sending it to the Cowboys to get back into the first round and select quarterback Brady Quinn.

The Browns went 10–6 in 2007, narrowly missing the playoffs, and appeared set to again be playoff contenders. On paper, the Browns' most glaring weakness was along the defensive line, and Savage didn't like what he saw from that year's draft class.

So he got aggressive at the March 2008 start of the league year, trading the Browns' 2008 second-round pick to the Packers for defensive tackle Corey Williams. The Browns gave Williams a six-year extension worth up to $38 million, with more than $16 million guaranteed. But Williams was never a great fit in coach Romeo Crennel's 3-4 defense, and it turned out to be anything but a great acquisition for the Browns.

The 2008 season and the Savage/Crennel era ended up as total busts. Williams was traded two years later in a swap of late-round draft picks.

Savage traded away the Browns' 2008 third-round pick for defensive tackle Shaun Rogers, who was one of the most talented players of the Browns' new era. But Rogers wasn't consistent, and the Browns found out why the Lions were willing to part with him. Rogers had rare athleticism for a man his size, made some splash plays, and was a gifted kick blocker, but he never consistently produced.

The draft was held over two days then, so the Browns didn't pick until Sunday afternoon. They had long targeted UNLV linebacker Beau Bell and got him in the fourth round, but Bell never turned into a player. His Browns career lasted all of five games.

The Browns made one outstanding pick in that 2008 Draft, sixth-round defensive tackle Ahtyba Rubin. Through 20 years of drafting in the new era, the Browns had averaged just seven starts per player drafted in the sixth round but they got 75 starts out of Rubin, who ended up playing in the NFL for more than a decade. Rubin and fullback Lawrence Vickers are the franchises' best sixth-round picks of the new era.

That led some to believe that Crennel had actually flipped a coin, which would have been wild even by Browns' standards.

The next season, when Donte Stallworth accidentally stepped on Braylon Edwards' foot as they horsed around after practice while Edwards wasn't wearing shoes, Crennel shrugged it off.

"Kids will be kids," he said. "They run around without their shoes on all the time."

Crennel was criticized for being too easy on the Browns in training camp in 2008, when they were coming off a 10-win season and prepping for the national spotlight and increased expectations. But he insisted that he needed healthy players to have a chance once the real games began, and injuries began to mount in the preseason. In the end, neither Anderson nor Brady Quinn played well enough at quarterback to win and the Browns finished that season with Ken Dorsey playing. A year after Crennel and other key members of the organizations got contract extensions, they got fired.

The Browns went 24–40 in Crennel's four seasons. Crennel is tied with his predecessor, Butch Davis (24–35), for the most wins by a coach in the team's new era.

Crennel later became head coach again with the Chiefs. There, he again had Quinn as his starting quarterback for a time. After being fired following the 2012 season, he took a year off from coaching before getting hired by the Texans, where he served as defensive coordinator and later was named assistant head coach. Crennel turned 72 in the summer of 2019, just before the start of his sixth season with the Texans.

59 Double the Magic

A Hail Mary rarely results in a big play. That Tim Couch completed two of them for game-winning touchdowns in the span of four seasons says that luck was on the new Browns' side, at least on occasion.

The new franchise scored its first win on October 31, 1999, in New Orleans when Couch lofted one high into the Superdome lights and it came down in the hands of Kevin Johnson along the sideline. Johnson positioned his feet and body well and appeared to believe all along that he had a shot at the play, which covered 56 yards as time expired to give the Browns a 21–16 win.

Couch removed his helmet and took a victory lap after the pass. Johnson and Couch, both 1999 draft picks, had connected on a 24-yard touchdown pass in the third quarter to give the Browns a 14–10 lead. The Browns moved to 1–7 with the win; their only other win that season also came with a bit of drama as Phil Dawson kicked a field goal as time expired in Pittsburgh.

In 2002, Couch and the Browns needed to win in Jacksonville in early December to stay in playoff contention. And they did, on the last play, when another Couch Hail Mary, this one covering 50 yards, moved the Browns to 7–6 on the season.

Quincy Morgan was nearly flat on his back when he reeled in the game-winning pass. The catch survived a lengthy replay review as the Jaguars believed Morgan had trapped it with help of the ground. Dawson's PAT kick wasn't a thing of beauty, but it went in and the Browns escaped with a 21–20 win in a game they ended up needing as they snuck in the playoffs.

In a strange nod to the first Hail Mary game with Johnson, Couch and Morgan had previously hooked up on a 60-yard

Tim Couch celebrates after throwing the 56-yard Hail Mary that beat the Saints, 21–16, on October 31, 1999. (Bill Feig/AP Photo)

touchdown pass in the third quarter, tying the game at 14. The Jaguars kicked two short field goals in the final three minutes, the second with 50 seconds left, to set up the game-winning drive and twice-in-a-lifetime pass.

Couch is the only quarterback in NFL history with two scoring passes of 50 yards or more with no time left on the clock, and that's a record that figures to stand for a long time.

60 From Out of Nowhere

The 2007 season started with a thud. It wasn't just that Charlie Frye won a training camp quarterback competition mostly by default. The Browns were a mess, and they got bullied by the Steelers in the opener, 34–7.

One of the lasting images of that game was fullback Lawrence Vickers celebrating his short touchdown catch from backup Derek Anderson in the third quarter—and Anderson sprinting into the end zone to tell Vickers to stop dancing with the Browns down by three scores. By the end, only towel-waving Steelers fans were left in Cleveland Browns Stadium.

The next day, Frye was traded. Yes, the very next day.

But the Browns recovered from that opening-day disaster and went on to win 10 games. Anderson threw for 3,787 yards, the most by a Browns quarterback in more than 20 years. Jamal Lewis became the only Browns runner not named Jim Brown to go over 1,300 yards in a season. Braylon Edwards and Kellen Winslow Jr. played to their draft position, and both joined Anderson in the Pro Bowl. Joe Jurevicius made his share of big catches, too.

"That team had some super-talented guys," Anderson said. "We could pound it in the run game with Jamal, and people forget how good [Lawrence] Vickers was as a fullback. He was a punisher. The line was good, too. I always felt I could have the time I needed to throw it deep. And Kellen and Braylon and Joe, they could catch the simple pass and turn it into big gains. We had a lot of pop.

"We made enough big plays that the confidence just kept growing. We thought we could make them all the time. We were never out of a game."

The Browns ran out of magic in games at Pittsburgh, Arizona, and Cincinnati, and they ultimately just missed the playoffs. But Joshua Cribbs was at his peak as a return man, and Phil Dawson kept making big kicks.

"The magic of that team was with the chemistry," punter Dave Zastudil said. "It was just belief. There was talent. There were a lot of older guys who had played on other teams, winning teams. And there was pedigree. Kellen and Braylon, those guys had all the talent in the world. It just took some time and some belief. Confidence and chemistry only come when you do it. Once we got some wins, guys knew we could play with anybody."

Cribbs had a 100-yard kick return touchdown at Pittsburgh on his way to leading the NFL with 1,809 kick return yards and a staggering 30.7 average.

"Obviously it was my job to know every returner and every return team in the league," Zastudil said. "There were faster guys. There were teams who set up incredible blocking schemes. But [Cribbs] was just different. He could make guys miss, but he'd also run through them. There'd be times that he maybe shouldn't have tried to return a ball but he did, and he'd bust one. He was fearless and he was tough to tackle. Every touch there was a chance he'd go a long way."

Edwards set a franchise record with 16 touchdown catches. He had a three-touchdown game in an October win over Miami, then caught eight passes for 117 yards and two touchdowns the next week as the Browns won in St. Louis.

"That team had a lot of talent," Jurevicius said. "Phil had added guys with experience, guys who could kind of lead the way. There were a lot of moving parts, still a lot of young guys early on. But it wasn't like one lightning strike. It was just a matter of timing, of eliminating the bad start and all the mess at quarterback. We could score on people a lot of different ways. Experience and belief are big things in the NFL, and we had both once everything kind of settled down."

61 Damn You, Denver

If you're a Browns fan, you know much of this book doesn't involve happy endings.

The old Browns had natural rivals in the Steelers and Bengals. But in the 1980s, the Browns lost three AFC Championship Games to the Broncos, two in heartbreaking fashion.

The 1986 Browns played and carried themselves like they were headed to the franchise's first Super Bowl, and they almost got there.

But John Elway and the Broncos drove 98 yards in 15 gut-wrenching plays, tying the AFC Championship Game with 37 seconds left. Elway threw a slant through traffic to Mark Jackson for a five-yard touchdown to tie it, and in overtime Rich Karlis just snuck a 33-yard field goal through the uprights for the win.

It's now known as The Drive. For decades, it played on loop during any big game involving a Cleveland sports team alongside

The Fumble, The Shot by Michael Jordan, and the Cleveland Indians' ninth-inning meltdown.

So, about The Fumble. The year after The Drive, the Browns were in Denver for the AFC Championship Game—and they were the team that needed a late drive. On January 17, 1988, the Browns trailed at halftime, 21–3. The Browns rallied to tie the game at 31 as Kosar threw three touchdown passes in the second half. Trailing 38–31 in the final minute, the Browns got to the Denver 8-yard line with 1:12 left. The Browns then fooled the Broncos with a draw play, and it looked like Earnest Byner would score.

But Broncos defensive back Jeremiah Castille saw Byner coming, and Castille ripped the ball out of Byner's hands at the 1-yard line. Byner never saw Castille coming, and Castille would say he went for the ball all the way. It worked. The Browns were crushed, and the Broncos went back to the Super Bowl.

The 1989 season again ended in Denver—again in the AFC Championship Game—with the Broncos pulling away from the Browns, 37–21.

Through 2018, the Broncos led the all-time series, 23–6. That the Browns won three of the first four games played from 1970 to '74 makes it even more lopsided in the memories of many fans.

In the first 20 seasons of the new era, there weren't many significant Browns-Broncos games. In 2006, a dominant win by the Broncos in Cleveland in a Sunday afternoon game led to Browns coach Romeo Crennel firing offensive coordinator Maurice Carthon.

In 2018, the Browns won a December Saturday night game in Denver that ended the Broncos' playoff chances. That was the Browns' first win in Denver since October 8, 1990, and the new-era Browns' first win over the Broncos in eight tries.

62 Life's a Snap

The first player drafted by the new-era Browns to be named to a Pro Bowl was long snapper Ryan Pontbriand. Though Pontbriand was good—and for a long time, near flawless—that's more an indictment of how the Browns drafted and how things went for the franchise before Pontbriand was picked for the Pro Bowl in 2007.

Though Butch Davis using a fifth-round pick on a long snapper was widely criticized when the Browns drafted him in 2003, Pontbriand was the Browns' long snapper for eight full seasons and much of a ninth before getting injured and retiring in 2011. He was also named to the Pro Bowl in 2008.

With Cribbs at his peak, the 2007 Browns team that went 10–6 was especially good on special teams. Dawson delivered two of his most memorable kicks in a 2007 road win at Baltimore, the first sending the game to overtime after players had left the field thinking the kick was no good. Replay review showed Dawson's 51-yard kick had gone through the uprights before hitting the stanchion and bouncing back into the field of play.

The Browns won the overtime coin toss, Cribbs returned the kickoff past the Ravens' 40-yard line, and after eight offensive plays, the Browns sent on the field goal team and Dawson split the uprights with a 33-yard field goal for a 33–30 win. In that game, the Ravens inexplicably kept kicking to Cribbs, who finished with 245 total kick return yards on seven returns.

Cribbs made the first of his three Pro Bowls after that 2007 season. He led the NFL with 1,809 kick return yards and a 30.7 average per return. He also returned a punt for a touchdown and led the NFL with 2,312 all-purpose yards. Cribbs was an All-Pro in 2009 after he posted three kick return touchdowns in addition to a punt return touchdown. He averaged an impressive 11.4 yards or greater on punt returns five times in his 10-year career, the first eight of which were played with the Browns.

From 2001 to 2015, only four true long snappers were drafted by NFL teams. That Pontbriand was second of the four says that his success helped those who came after him. In 2017, the Browns made long snapper Charley Hughlett the league's highest-paid long snapper with a six-year extension that averaged over $1 million per season.

63 The Legend of Benjamin Gay

The running joke about the Butch Davis–led personnel department wasn't that funny. Because Davis and his right-hand man, Pete Garcia, had done such a good job using every possible avenue to find and recruit talent to the University of Miami, they tried to use those same methods with the Browns.

Minor league baseball players, failed former blue-chip recruits, and other resurrection projects were welcome with the Browns. Most of them just weren't much help against the Ravens and Steelers.

The most memorable—and probably the most talented—of them all was running back Benjamin Gay, who'd been so good as a Texas high school star that he earned the nickname "The Legend." But Gay had legendary baggage that included trouble going to class and fulfilling other obligations, so he ended up in junior college and then had a short stint in the CFL that ended so poorly that he owed his agent money. When Gay went through the Supplemental

Draft without being picked, the Browns signed him at the start of training camp in 2001.

And it was obvious rather quickly that Gay could really run. He broke a long run in the team's first scrimmage, and fans adopted him as a lovable underdog. He told stories to reporters about dealing drugs and being in gang shootouts in junior college, and he told them with a smile. Gay said he was ready to make the most of his chances, and he was so good in the preseason that the Browns had to keep him.

He was never a full-time player, but in a game against the vaunted Ravens defense, Gay fell down as he was taking a handoff. He got up, spun away from a tackle, reversed field, and turned the play into a big gain. During practice he'd break into the open field and coaches and personnel execs on the sideline would look like they'd just seen a ghost.

The Browns listed Gay at 6-foot-1, 227. He had long, powerful strides. He didn't shy away from contact but had at least somewhat of an extra gear to get past pursuers. He had all the talent in the world. He just struggled to show up on time, to stay focused, to stay on top of the playbook. He lasted just one season with the Browns, and after the Colts claimed him on waivers he didn't show up. They cut him, too, and he never played again.

Gay's career stat line ended like this: 51 carries for 172 yards, one touchdown, and 55 total touches highlighted by one spectacular 40-yard run.

Travis Prentice, a 2000 draft pick at running back who correctly figured that Gay would take his roster spot, made a hilarious observation as he strolled through the locker room one day during training camp and saw a gaggle of reporters at Gay's locker.

"It's hard being a legend," Prentice said.

For Gay, it was too hard to sustain.

64 Hard Knocks

Keeping Hue Jackson as coach for the 2018 season meant the Browns were eligible for *Hard Knocks*, the all-access reality series produced each summer by HBO and NFL Films.

A crew of more than 30 full-time employees was on site with the Browns for the duration of training camp and preseason. Their job was to capture everything they could, from the meeting rooms to the locker room to the practice field. The Browns had right of first refusal only when it came to making sure the show didn't share potential strategic information such as play designs or snap counts.

The cameras were there when the Browns traded Corey Coleman, a first-round bust who had fallen out of the lineup. The cameras followed undrafted players chasing their NFL dreams. The cameras caught a little-known running backs coach named Freddie Kitchens standing up to Jackson in a staff meeting, essentially saying that players being given a day off should at least be in uniform as the Browns were setting a bad tone by being so liberal in handing out camp off days.

Offensive coordinator Todd Haley backed Kitchens, telling Jackson the Browns had "a bunch of players who haven't done shit out there not doing shit." Jackson's response was basically that he was the boss and was going to do things his way.

Five months later, Kitchens was the boss. Both Haley and Jackson were fired at midseason, and after rookie quarterback Baker Mayfield excelled in the second half of the season with Kitchens calling the plays, the Browns promoted him from interim offensive coordinator to full-time head coach.

Hard Knocks made Jackson seem like an insecure egomaniac. The cameras rarely lie. Determined not to have a quarterback competition, Jackson didn't give Mayfield a single rep with the No. 1 offense through training camp. In one particularly memorable scene, quarterback Tyrod Taylor was seen and heard giving Jackson coaching tips when it came to calling out players giving less than maximum effort.

In a tirade at least partially directed at Coleman, wide receiver Jarvis Landry lit up the wide receiver room with a rant about the importance of players not skipping practice and taking their jobs seriously.

"All that weak shit don't live here no more," Landry said. "That shit don't exist. That's contagious, bruh."

A Hard Knocks *crew films a drill during Browns training camp on July 28, 2018, in Berea, Ohio.* (Frank Jansky/Icon Sportswire/Getty Images)

Per NFL rules, the Browns don't have to do *Hard Knocks* again for a long time. Teams see it as invasive and a distraction, but fans see the show as a raw and rare look inside. The Browns went into 2019 hoping winning would stay contagious and that they could maintain a national profile without inviting 30 cameras inside their walls.

65 Charlie Frye

The Browns never saw Charlie Frye as their franchise quarterback. But they drafted him in the third round in 2005 because they liked Frye's competitiveness and playmaking ability, and they believed he had a chance to someday become a starting-quality quarterback.

Frye had grown up in Willard, Ohio, about 75 miles southwest of Cleveland. He starred at the University of Akron and was named MVP of the Senior Bowl. The Browns were starting the Phil Savage–Romeo Crennel era in 2005. Trent Dilfer was the placeholder quarterback, and wide receiver Braylon Edwards was the No. 3 overall pick. It made sense that the next priority would have been to find the franchise quarterback to get the ball to Edwards and maybe Kellen Winslow Jr., the first-round pick in 2004 who wrecked his knee in a motorcycle accident not long after the 2005 Draft.

Frye started the last five games as a rookie and was the starter the next season. The Browns weren't good, and though Frye completed 64 percent of his passes in 2006 he was sacked 44 times and threw 17 interceptions. No one questioned his toughness, but it was becoming clear he wasn't the long-term answer. Frye was injured late in the 2006 season, and in the 2007 Draft the Browns traded back into the first round to take another Ohio-born quarterback, Brady Quinn.

One story explains how ready the Browns—and their fans—were for a transition to Quinn.

In the summer of 2007, Cleveland Browns Stadium hosted a day-long concert headlined by country star Kenny Chesney. Frye showed up with some friends and was spotted by a group of fans to the right of the stage. From where Frye was standing at the time, he couldn't see the stage.

Jennifer Nettles, lead singer of the band Sugarland, came out late in her group's set wearing a No. 10 Brady Quinn jersey. When fans cheered enthusiastically for Nettles and her Quinn jersey, Frye waved back, believing the cheers were for him.

Frye won a training-camp competition for the starting job in 2007 but was benched during the opening game and traded the day after the opener. He ended up starting 19 games for the Browns and then started four more, one for the Seahawks in 2008 and three the following year for the Raiders, including one against the Browns in Cleveland as the 2009 Browns finished the year on a four-game win streak.

Frye got into coaching after his playing career. He started in high school, calling plays under former Browns teammate Kenard Lang in Florida. He later was on staffs at the University of Florida and Ashland University before landing at Central Michigan as quarterbacks coach and offensive coordinator in 2019.

66 Big Money, Little Return

In 2001, new coach Butch Davis went against the advice of his scouts and the grading of the pre-draft process. With the No. 3 pick in the draft, Davis and the Browns selected defensive tackle Gerard Warren out of the University of Florida.

He already had the nickname "Big Money" before he showed up overweight for his first offseason program. Warren got a $12 million signing bonus from the Browns after holding out and missing the first 15 practices to start training camp.

His production never matched the nickname. Warren was athletic for a man who played in the neighborhood of 320 pounds and made the occasional splash play, but he's probably best remembered for getting arrested two hours away in Pittsburgh in November of his rookie season for carrying an unlicensed firearm.

In addressing the arrest later that week, Browns team president Carmen Policy said Pittsburgh police told him Warren "was the nicest guy they ever arrested."

It was heartwarming, really. In 2004, Warren was doing an interview and was asked about the Browns' plan to slow Steelers quarterback Ben Roethslisberger, who was in the midst of an outstanding rookie season.

"One rule they used to tell me," Warren said. "Kill the head and the body's dead."

That didn't quite work for the Browns. Warren got a formal warning from the NFL office about watching his language and watching his actions regarding Roethlisberger. In his rookie season, Warren had been fined $35,000 by the NFL for a high hit on Jaguars quarterback Mark Brunell following a Browns' interception.

Late in that 2004 season, the resignation of Davis put Warren back in the spotlight—even when Warren's play did not warrant it. Interim coach Terry Robiskie vowed to "make Warren a better person," even if he couldn't make him a better player. During one meeting with reporters, Warren was asked if he'd thought about the Browns moving on from him.

"There are 31 other teams who might want me," he said.

Then, he was asked what would happen if none of those other teams were interested.

"We'll go back to Florida and hang out," he said.

Warren was traded in March 2005 to the Broncos for a fourth-round pick. He actually made it seven more years before going back to Florida to hang out. Warren played two seasons with the Broncos, then three with the Raiders before finishing his career by playing 2010–11 with the Patriots. Warren finished his career with 36.5 sacks, seven forced fumbles, and five fumble recoveries.

67 Playing Spoiler

Browns-Bengals games always have significance, even though both franchises have gone through their share of difficult times. And more than their share, too.

Bengals owner Mike Brown still holds a grudge for the firing of his father, Paul, even though Art Modell last owned the Browns in 1995. The in-state rivalry always makes for good fan and family fodder. In 1989, Bengals coach Sam Wyche took the microphone after being asked to address the crowd about throwing objects on to the field and told the Riverfront Stadium fans, "You don't live in Cleveland! You live in Cincinnati."

Also, Browns fans wish the Bengals would have just followed through with a proposed idea to make Hue Jackson their coach in-waiting behind Marvin Lewis. But Jackson left in 2016 to become head coach of the Browns, and the rest is NFL history.

Anyway, back to the field. The wild, high-scoring shootouts of the 2004 and 2007 seasons are among the most fun games of the first 20 years of the Browns' new era. The Bengals probably thought Johnny Manziel's debut as starter in 2014 was pretty fun, too, considering they won, 30–0.

But the two most significant Browns-Bengals games of the new era, as far as the standings, both took place in December in Cincinnati. The 2003 Browns were 4–11 headed into the season finale, and the Browns really were headed nowhere. The Bengals were 8–7 and needed to win to keep their playoff hopes alive in the first season under Lewis.

The Browns showed up with an inspired effort and kept the Bengals out of the postseason thanks to a big game from rookie running back Lee Suggs, who rushed for 186 yards and two touchdowns, including a career-long 78-yarder in the second quarter as the Browns took control.

Suggs put the Browns ahead for good with 7:44 left in what became a 22–14 win.

If the Browns had saved some of that run-first attack for their December 23, 2007, visit to Cincinnati, they likely would have won and made the playoffs. The Browns were 9–5 at the time and the Bengals were 5–9, but the Bengals jumped out to a 19–0 lead in the second quarter and held on to win, 19–14.

Derek Anderson threw 48 passes, and though two of them went to Braylon Edwards for second-half touchdowns as the Browns tried to fight back, four of them went to the Bengals.

The wind was gusting that day. Offensive coordinator Chudzinski hurt the Browns with his insistence on a pass-heavy attack rather than letting Jamal Lewis drive the offense. Lewis got 92 yards on 21 carries, but the Browns had just 25 rushing attempts.

Trailing by five, the Browns forced a fumble with 1:48 left and needed to drive 83 yards to win. Anderson immediately hit Edwards for what appeared to be a gain of 41 yards, but Edwards was flagged for offensive interference and the Browns were backed up inside their own 10-yard line. They got all the way to the Bengals' 29 in the closing seconds, but Anderson's desperation heave for Kellen Winslow Jr. was broken up by Johnathan Joseph.

68 Zeus Goes Wild

One of the most bizarre incidents in NFL history took place in the Browns' first season back in the NFL.

On December 19, 1999, the Browns were hosting the Jaguars when a penalty flag tossed by referee Jeff Triplette somehow got between the top of Orlando Brown's helmet and his facemask and struck Brown in the right eye. Brown immediately went down. Eventually he got up and left the field, but soon he came back, shouting at Triplette and eventually shoving him to the ground.

Brown was ejected. He then kicked over yard markers on his way out. Fans cheered his fit of rage, unaware that he'd been seriously injured and was temporarily blinded.

Brown, nicknamed "Zeus" because he was one of the league's largest players at listed measurements at 6-foot-7, 360 pounds, played for the original Browns in 1995, then the Ravens before returning to Cleveland in 1999. That made him a fan favorite, but that would be the last game he'd play for the Browns.

The NFL initially handed Brown an indefinite suspension for assaulting an official, but relented when it was discovered that Brown had serious eye damage. Brown spoke out against Triplette for years after the incident, acknowledging it was a freak accident but maintaining that the referee did not need to throw the flag the way he did.

In 2001, Brown sued the NFL for $200 million. According to reports, he settled for a sum between $15 million and $25 million in 2002.

Though he didn't play from the day of the accident until 2003 and was released by the Browns in 2000, Brown returned to play for the Ravens in 2003 and was a starter for the Ravens until he retired after playing nine games in 2005. He started 119 of 129 career games, playing almost exclusively at right tackle.

Brown died in 2011 at 40. His son, Orlando Brown Jr., was drafted by the Ravens in 2018. He also plays offensive tackle.

69 Pick Parties

The franchise's all-time interception leaders put up eye-popping numbers long before football became a pass-happy game. Thom Darden had 45 interceptions in 128 games across nine seasons, while Warren Lahr had 40 interceptions in 114 games from 1949 to 1959, playing in both the AAFC and the NFL.

Darden, a safety, grew up in Sandusky, Ohio, and was the Browns' first-round pick in 1972 after playing collegiately at Michigan. He was named to the Pro Bowl in 1978 after leading the NFL with 10 interceptions. Lahr played on three NFL championship teams and one AAFC championship team

The Browns have an impressive defensive back lineage, but the only Hall of Famer who played defensive back for the Browns is Don Shula, who was elected to the Hall for his coaching career with the Dolphins. Shula played for the Browns in 1951–52.

Probably the franchise's most popular cornerbacks are credited with starting the "Dawg Pound" concept that spans Browns history from the 1980s to the new era. Hanford Dixon played for the Browns from 1981 to '89. He had 26 career interceptions, went to three Pro Bowls, and was twice named All-Pro. Frank Minnifield played for the Browns from 1984 to 1992, making four Pro Bowls and earning first-team All-Pro honors in 1988.

Safety Eric Turner is considered to be one of the most talented defenders in franchise history. The No. 2 overall pick in the 1991 Draft was big, rangy, and delivered highlight-reel hits to receivers both of the suspecting and unsuspecting variety. An All-Pro in 1994 after leading the NFL with nine interceptions, Turner had 17 interceptions in five seasons with the Browns. He went on to play one year with the Ravens after the franchise moved, then finished his career by playing three years with the Raiders. Turner died in 2000 of stomach cancer. He was 31.

Turner played collegiately at UCLA, as did another talented former Browns safety, Don Rogers. The Browns selected Rogers with pick No. 18 in the 1984 Draft, and Rogers was named NFL Defensive Rookie of the Year. But he played just one more season. In the summer of 1986, Rogers died of a cocaine overdose. He was just 23.

Bernie Kosar would later call Rogers "one of the most magnificent football players that God ever created. No disrespect to Ronnie Lott or anyone else, but Rogers was big. He was strong, he was fast, he was fantastic."

Anthony Henry had the best statistical cornerback season of the new era when the fourth-round pick intercepted 10 passes as a rookie in 2001, tying for the most in the NFL that season. Henry was a rangy, long-armed cornerback who had three of those 10 interceptions in one game as the Browns tied a franchise record with seven interceptions against the Lions on September 23, 2001.

Later that season he returned an interception 97 yards for a touchdown against the Jaguars. Henry played four years with the Browns, then played four with the Cowboys and one with the Lions. He finished his career with 31 interceptions.

Through 20 seasons of the new era, 2010 first-round pick Joe Haden was the interception leader with 19. Henry was next with 17. Next on the list were two safeties, Tashaun Gipson and Sean Jones, each with 14.

Cornerback Daylon McCutcheon, a 1999 draft pick who became the first drafted player of the new era to sign a second contract with the team, had 12 interceptions in his seven seasons with the Browns. Leigh Bodden, an undrafted success story who became the Browns' No. 1 cornerback in the mid-2000s, also had 12 interceptions in his five seasons with the Browns.

The Browns used the No. 4 overall pick in the 2018 NFL Draft on cornerback Denzel Ward, who'd grown up in nearby Summit County and played at Ohio State. Ward was young—he turned 21 the day after the Browns drafted him—and athletic, and he forced two turnovers in his first NFL game vs. the Steelers. Despite dealing with some injury issues later in his rookie season, Ward was named to the Pro Bowl and played well enough to stamp himself as a potential future star.

70 William Green's Winding Journey

William Green's success with the Browns didn't last, but the only playoff appearance of the first 20 years of the team's new era would not have happened without Green's powerful and assertive running late in his rookie season.

The No. 16 pick in the 2002 Draft ran for 726 yards in the final seven games of his rookie season. His 64-yard touchdown in the season finale against the Falcons lives in team lore thanks to the Browns sneaking into the playoffs and longtime play-by-play man Jim Donovan's call of "Run, William, run!"

Despite a slow start to his rookie year, Green finished 2002 with 887 yards and six touchdowns and looked like he'd be a key piece of a young and improving offense going forward. Early in 2003, he served as the workhorse back as the Browns scored their first victory in Heinz Field, then the new home of the Steelers, and stamped themselves as AFC North contenders. But things unraveled quickly, for the team and for the talented but troubled young runner.

About midway through that second year, Green was suspended four games for violating the NFL's substance abuse policy. Green was arrested for drunk driving and marijuana possession during the suspension; he was barely wearing any clothing while driving through a Cleveland suburb in the middle of the afternoon when police pulled him over.

A few weeks later, he was stabbed by his then-fiancé, Asia Gray, during a domestic dispute. Green initially lied to police and to Browns officials about the incident, saying he'd been injured in an accident and had fallen on a knife. The Browns almost released

Green after that incident; his fiancé was eventually charged with felonious assault.

Green played two more years for the Browns, who used his circumstances in pushing the NFL to change its rules regarding suspended players not being allowed in the team facility. The Browns argued that troubled players needed structure and support, and that eventual change would pop up again later for the Browns with Josh Gordon. But after all the drama, Green was never the same player. He ran for 585 yards in 2004, then played sparingly in 2005.

The Browns knew Green had issues, but despite Butch Davis' penchant for taking Miami players, the Browns chose to draft Green and not safety Ed Reed, who went on to a Hall of Fame career with the Ravens. Davis had coached against Green at Boston College and saw him as a rare runner capable of carrying an offense in less-than-ideal Cleveland weather conditions.

By the time he was 13, Green had lost both of his parents to AIDS. Green had issues with drinking and drugs—before, during, and after his NFL career. He was suspended twice during his college career for marijuana use.

Davis used to insist that Green was a good person who was shy and susceptible because he'd been through so much in his life. Later, Green got sober and admitted in multiple interviews that his life had been "a complete mess" for a long time, including when he was with the Browns.

More than a decade after his career ended, Green was working as a youth minister and motivational speaker. He got married to Asia Gray, his high school sweetheart, and the couple had three children.

71 Slump Busters

Though the new Browns have been mostly terrible with their first-round draft picks since returning to the league, in 2009 and 2010 they drafted players who would become Pro Bowlers.

Eric Mangini's only draft in charge started with a bunch of trades but led to the Browns drafting Alex Mack, who became a key part of some strong offensive lines and made a Pro Bowl. He later made multiple Pro Bowls and played in a Super Bowl with the Falcons.

The best cornerback of the team's new era has been Joe Haden, the Browns' first-round pick in 2010. Haden had a big rookie season with six interceptions and immediately became a fan favorite. He was not afraid to come up and help in the run game, and he immediately showed some of the same pass-coverage skills that the league's top cornerbacks possessed.

The 2010 Browns were one of the most interesting teams of the new era. Like many other Browns teams, they ultimately didn't have enough offense to contend and went forward enduring change while looking for a quarterback. But that was Tom Heckert's first year as general manager, and Mike Holmgren's first year getting paid big bucks to occasionally call the shots. And though it became Mangini's last season, the Browns were clearly better in their second year under Mangini.

The season highlight was a dominating win over the Patriots. That was the biggest game for Peyton Hillis, who went from little-used fullback with the Broncos to rushing for 1,177 yards and 11 touchdowns with the Browns in 2010. Hillis was voted to the cover of the popular Madden video game the next year, but he squabbled with the Browns over his contract, played in only 10 games, and was gone by 2012.

Change was the only constant—Heckert and Holmgren knew they were out the moment the Haslam family took ownership in 2012—but Haden and Mack joined Joe Thomas in a small group of first-round success stories.

Haden was named to the Pro Bowl in both 2013 and 2014 and for a long time was a leader in an ever-changing Browns locker room. Haden was a popular player who was active in the community. He often acted as the team spokesman as the Browns endured tough times and sweeping changes. Injuries took their toll, and Haden's play fell off in 2015–16.

With Haden entering the last year of his deal in 2017, the Sashi Brown–led front office made the decision to release Haden at the end of the preseason. The Browns couldn't find a trade partner for Haden because of the money left on his contract and his lingering injury issues, but he was under contract for that season and there was no real reason outside of front-office arrogance for the Browns to cut one of their better players.

The move did not play well in the locker room or with then-coach Hue Jackson, but the Browns cut Haden anyway and he immediately signed a three-year contract with the Steelers. After two productive seasons with the Steelers, the team re-worked his contract to keep him on board despite Haden turning 30 before the 2019 season.

72 Cribbs Unleashed

Joshua Cribbs' best moment came in the Browns' 2007 game at Pittsburgh when Cribbs' bobbed and weaved through the Steelers, setting up his blocks and making a couple would-be tacklers look silly en route to a 100-yard kickoff return for the ages. The Browns took the lead, 28–24, on that return with 11:14 to play but ultimately lost the game.

But that wasn't Cribbs' best overall game. To pick that would require a choice among three: Cribbs' big game in Baltimore earlier in that 2007 season; his 269-yard, two-touchdown game in Kansas City in 2009; and another tough-to-tackle performance against the Steelers in a brutally cold 2009 home game.

All three were vintage Cribbs. He ran fearlessly and powerfully. It sometimes wasn't pretty and generally was off-script, but Cribbs had a knack for finding daylight and escaping tackles, even when it looked like he might fumble or go backwards 10 yards along the way.

In that game in Baltimore, Cribbs amassed 245 yards in the return game. The Ravens kept kicking to him, a decision that led to Brian Billick getting fired at the end of the season. When a famous Phil Dawson field goal changed via replay review sent the game to overtime, the Ravens inexplicably kicked to Cribbs again. He returned the kick 41 yards, putting the Browns a couple easy passes away from the winning field goal.

That game in Kansas City is best remembered for Jerome Harrison going from backup to franchise record holder after Harrison ran for 286 yards and three second-half touchdowns. But Cribbs kept the Browns in the game and set the stage for Harrison with kickoff return touchdowns of 100 and 103 yards in the first half. Cribbs got three carries and caught a pass in that game in addition to racking up 269 kick return yards and 36 punt return yards.

That game came a week after Cribbs had played quarterback, running back, and returned a punt 55 yards in an upset of the Steelers that ended the Steelers' playoff hopes. Playing on a brutally cold Thursday night in Cleveland, Cribbs went back to his college days as a read-option quarterback and ran for 87 yards. He'd draw the defense and hand off to one-hit wonder Chris Jennings, who ran for 73 yards and a touchdown that night.

In 2009, Cribbs was the Browns' third-leading rusher and seventh-leading receiver despite being a utility player. That year's offense wasn't exactly loaded with Pro Bowl talent, but Cribbs' explosion and versatility made it hard to keep him off the field. He was the NFL's most dangerous return man for a long time, and as stubborn opponents kept giving him chances he kept producing big plays.

73 The Curse of the No. 22 Pick

Phil Savage used to say that the Browns couldn't waste a second worrying about bad luck or believing that new organization was cursed. That, Savage said, would be a waste of time.

He was right. But from staph infections to motorcycle accidents to losing on a helmet toss as time expired, the new-era Browns have had enough crappy luck for six franchises. From LeCharles Bentley's injury that led to Bentley almost losing his leg to a staph infection to William Green going from conquering hero to getting stabbed by his girlfriend, all the way to a wide-open

Corey Coleman dropping a sure touchdown to complete an 0–16 season, luck has not often been on the side of the new-era Browns.

The Browns made their share of bad draft picks, too, specifically at the quarterback position.

Brady Quinn was such a popular pick at No. 22 in 2007 that the team's website servers were shut down for hours after the pick was made. Quinn never really did much on the field, though, and was traded after his third season. He held out in 2007, never played much of a role in the Charlie Frye–Derek Anderson quarterback competition that summer, and was traded away after two years of the Browns bouncing between Anderson and Quinn with little success.

Brandon Weeden was the No. 22 pick in 2012. He started immediately but made it just two seasons and is probably best remembered for getting stuck under the giant American flag during the National Anthem before his first game. You can't make this stuff up.

Johnny Manziel was the No. 22 pick in 2014. The thought that Manziel is the worst pick in franchise history is a legitimate one. One of the few counterarguments to that is that Manziel was the second of two first-round picks the Browns made that year. Justin Gilbert didn't have the fame Manziel had, but he produced little on the field and also was in trouble off of the field.

It's difficult—and probably unfair—to compare any recent draft pick to Manziel. So, apologies to Weeden and Quinn. But all of those picks contributed to the thought that the Browns were just doomed, and that the No. 22 pick should be avoided going forward.

Many in the Browns' personnel department knew the Manziel pick was a bad idea, but owner Jimmy Haslam pushed it anyway. Manziel was a celebrity quarterback who only put much effort into being a celebrity. After two seasons of Manziel mostly embarrassing the team off the field and not doing much on it, the Browns cut Manziel.

Weeden also made it just two years with the Browns. He had a strong arm but had terrible footwork and wasn't very accurate. Without going through an extensive scouting report, he never had a chance as a starting quarterback. There was no explaining or

The Curse of the No. 22 Pick continued—or culminated—with the doomed selection of Johnny Manziel in 2014. (Elsa/Staff/Getty Images)

Bad Billy

Johnny Manziel had all sorts of stunts in his time with the Browns, most of them related to partying and blowing off his football responsibilities. Most of them really aren't funny considering the multiple times Manziel sought treatment for substance abuse and was arrested for assaulting his then-girlfriend.

The Browns on at least one occasion had to send team staffers to Manziel's residence to wake him up. There's the story of how, ahead of his rookie season, Manziel was dining with business manager Maverick Carter when some fans approached and told Manziel they hoped he'd win the starting job that summer.

"I will," Manziel told them between sips. "I mean, I'm going against Brian Hoyer."

In his second season, the Browns announced Manziel as their starter during the team's bye week. But then Manziel went back to Texas and again showed up on social media partying. He'd promised coach Mike Pettine he wouldn't do that, so Pettine had to bench him again.

But the most egregious and entitled Manziel move came before the 2015 season finale. Manziel had been placed on injured reserve due to a concussion, but still had mandatory treatment sessions and meetings to attend. On the day before the last game vs. the Steelers, Manziel booked a noon flight to Las Vegas with the intention—at least he says—of returning that night.

Instead, he stayed in Las Vegas, donning a costume and telling people his name was "Billy." Knowing he'd been recognized, Manziel made an Instagram post and tagged it Avon, Ohio, where he lived. He missed his flight and missed the game the next day. And so Billy Manziel became the last, sad chapter in Johnny Manziel's two disastrous seasons with the Browns.

"I got back to the room at three or four in the morning," Manziel later said on the Joe Thomas–Andrew Hawkins podcast. "It's already 7:00 AM East Coast time, and we play [the Steelers] at one. I have to be there [for concussion treatment] at eight, which is in an hour. I just turn my phone off and throw it in the drawer and, 'We'll figure it out when we wake up.'"

On the same podcast in 2018, Manziel said he'd gotten sober and regretted his lack of respect for the NFL and his teammates during his short stint in Cleveland.

"It's to the point in time where I'm able to look back, reflect, know that it was a mistake, know that I made some really childish, immature decisions," Manziel said. "This decision that I made, what a complete lack of respect for guys like Joe Thomas. What a complete lack of respect for an organization that was trying to stick by me even with having a concussion at this point in time. What a completely selfish decision."

justifying that pick, which summed up the Mike Holmgren Era for the Browns. Holmgren took a lot of then-owner Randy Lerner's money and delivered little. In his final formal press conference after Jimmy Haslam bought the team, Holmgren said he believed that the Browns had finally found their quarterback in Weeden.

In 2007, the Browns traded back into the first round and selected Quinn. By that time, the Browns knew that Frye wasn't their long-term answer. That draft started with Joe Thomas, who will end up in the Hall of Fame, but the Quinn pick never worked out despite Quinn's popularity. Quinn made 12 starts for the Browns, winning just three.

In fairness, not all the No. 22 picks have been bad. In 1981, the Browns used the No. 22 pick on a cornerback out of Southern Mississippi. Hanford Dixon played his whole career in Cleveland, starred on some of the most memorable teams in franchise history, and went to three Pro Bowls. Dixon was inducted into the Cleveland Browns Legends in 2003, the third year the program was instituted.

74 The Pass Catchers

Pun intended, Jim Brown is the runaway leader among the franchise's running backs. The margin isn't as wide when it comes to catching passes, but tight end Ozzie Newsome is clearly the franchise's receiving leader.

Newsome had 7,980 yards in 198 career games from 1978 to 1990. Next is Dante Lavelli, an original Cleveland Brown and Northeast Ohio native, with 6,488. Another original Brown, Mac Speedie, is third with 5,602. Also over 5,000 yards for their respective careers with the Browns were Ray Renfro (5,508), Gary Collins (5,299), and Paul Warfield (5,210).

Though he did it twice, Newsome shares the franchise single-season record of 89 receptions with Kellen Winslow Jr. Newsome's streak of 150 consecutive games with at least one pass reception, a streak that stretched from 1979 to 1989, stood as the second-longest in NFL history at the time. Newsome caught 50 or more passes in six seasons, had three or more receptions in 112 games and eight or more catches 13 times.

Newsome is joined in the Hall of Fame by Warfield and Lavelli. Lavelli had 62 touchdown catches with the Browns, and Warfield had 52.

Collins is the franchise's all-time leader with 70 touchdown catches. A two-time Pro Bowler who also was the punter for much of his 10-year career, Collins played on the 1964 NFL Championship team and was selected to the Pro Bowl in both 1965 and 1966.

Through 20 years, Braylon Edwards and Josh Gordon were the best receivers of the new era. Edwards wasn't consistently great but he was dominant for much of 2007, when he caught a franchise-record

16 touchdown passes. He posted 3,697 receiving yards with the Browns and scored 28 touchdowns from 2005 to '09.

Gordon's star-crossed, suspension-shortened run with the Browns ended in 2018, but he was good enough to lead the NFL and set the franchise record with 1,646 receiving yards in 14 games in 2013. Kevin Johnson is the new era leader in receptions (315) and yards (3,836). He scored 23 receiving touchdowns in five seasons.

75 Brief Glimpses

The Browns built a nice receiving corps in the early 2000s via the second round. For a brief period, Kevin Johnson, Quincy Morgan, Dennis Northcutt, and Andre Davis were good enough that the four of them were on the cover of the team's media guide in 2003, which at the time was a pretty high honor.

But Johnson didn't survive that season with the Browns. Morgan ended up getting traded the next season. Tim Couch never really built on his breakout 2002 season, and 2003 ended up being Couch's final NFL season. Kelly Holcomb was magical in the 2002 playoff game and pedestrian after that.

Johnson was drafted in the second round in 1999 and was Couch's first favorite target. Johnson caught eight touchdown passes as a rookie and nine in 2001 before the Browns beefed up the receiving corps, his production started to slip and he was cut after beefing with then-coach Butch Davis. Johnson was benched in November 2003, then cut the next week. Johnson claimed he was blind-sided by the move, while Davis insisted that the Browns had asked Johnson for more as a blocker and had higher overall expectations.

On the field, the younger and faster receivers were making more plays. Off the field, it was a ramping-up of the Davis power play that didn't end well for Davis or the Browns.

Johnson was the No. 32 pick, the first pick in the second round. His 84 catches in 2001 are the fifth-most in a single season in team history.

Northcutt was picked in the same No. 32 spot the year after Johnson was. While Northcutt is best remembered for his drop that likely would have clinched the 2002 playoff game in Pittsburgh, he had a long and productive NFL career. He played seven years for the Browns, catching 276 passes for 3,438 yards and 11 touchdowns. He was the team's primary punt returner for most of those years, and in 2002 he led the NFL with two punt return touchdowns. He averaged 10.6 yards per return for his Browns career.

Morgan caught the Hail Mary pass from Couch to give the new Browns one of their most memorable early wins in 2002 in Jacksonville, capping a rally that kept the Browns' playoff hopes alive. Morgan was the No. 33 pick of the 2001 Draft. Andre Davis, who had played against the Butch Davis–led Miami teams in college, was the No. 47 pick in 2002.

The speedy Andre Davis caught the franchise-record 99-yard touchdown pass from Jeff Garcia in the 2004 October win over the Bengals. That helped Davis average a staggering 26 yards per reception in what became an injury-shortened 2004 season for him. He had 11 touchdown catches over his first two seasons but was traded to the Patriots in 2005. Davis played five more seasons, mostly as a backup with the Patriots, Bills, and Texans.

During that 2002 playoff season, Johnson led the team in receptions but Morgan led in yards and touchdowns. With the help of that 50-yard Hail Mary, Morgan was first leaguewide among eligible pass-catchers in 2002 at an average of 17.2 yards per reception. He, too, was later shipped out after his attitude became an issue, getting traded to the Cowboys for Antonio Bryant in 2004.

Morgan won a Super Bowl with the Steelers as a backup in 2005 but never caught a pass after that.

76 Monday Night Football

Monday Night Football was born in Cleveland on September 21, 1970. The Browns beat the Joe Namath–led Jets that night, 31–21. A 94-yard kickoff return touchdown by Homer Jones was the biggest play, and a Billy Andrews interception return of a Namath pass provided the exclamation point.

Long before the average consumer had 300 TV channels and sometimes as many as six nights of football per week, *Monday Night Football* games were special. But in the early days they were considered a risk for ABC and the NFL. *Monday Night Football* was a big leap from the norm.

But it worked, and the rise of *Monday Night Football* through the 1970s and 1980s was a large part of the NFL's rise as it showcased the NFL's best players and best teams. From 1987 to 1990, the Browns played eight times on Monday night, including marquee games against the Broncos, Oilers, and Dolphins. Then and now, the best quarterback matchups generally become the best TV matchups.

The new-era Browns first played on Monday night in 2003, a home loss to the Rams. The Browns didn't earn another Monday night game until 2008, when Braylon Edwards did a backflip, a cartwheel, then scored a touchdown. Cornerback Eric Wright high-stepped into the end zone on an interception return, and the Browns ended up pulling away from the Giants, the defending Super Bowl champions.

Just how bad things got for the Browns starting in 2008 and lasting for a decade can be explained as such: Joe Thomas played in just five Monday night games in his 11-year Hall of Fame career. Three of them were in his second season when the Browns went 4–12 but got half of those wins on Monday night, beating the Giants and later going on the road and beating the Bills, 29–27. Late in that season the Browns with Ken Dorsey at quarterback were blown out in Philadelphia, 30–10.

The Browns got one *Monday Night Football* game the following year. After losing that game to the Ravens, 16–0, they did not get another Monday night game until 2015. That home game vs. the Ravens goes down as especially bizarre and deflating, even by new Browns' standards. The Browns lined up for a game-winning field goal in the closing seconds, but the 51-yard attempt by Travis Coons was blocked by Brent Urban and returned 64 yards for a touchdown by Will Hill, giving the Ravens a stunning 33–27 victory.

When the Browns got two Monday night games on their 2019 schedule—one at the Jets as sort of a celebration 50 seasons after *Monday Night Football* was born—it marked just the second time in the decade they'd played on Monday night. The hot finish to the 2018 season coupled with the addition of Odell Beckham Jr, gave the 2019 Browns four national TV night games on their initial schedule.

In their first 20 years back in the league, the new-era Browns were 8–16 in primetime games played on Sunday, Monday, Thursday, or Saturday nights. That brought the franchise's all-time record in such games to 24–32.

In the mid-2000s, *Sunday Night Football* began to replace *Monday Night Football* as the marquee game of the week. NBC took over Sunday night rights in 2006, ending a two-decade run for ESPN. With the move, ESPN took over Monday night games and the NFL implemented flex scheduling in Weeks 10–15.

Because Monday and Thursday night games can't be moved on short notice for multiple logistical reasons, the NFL started shifting Sunday night games to ensure significant games—and those with the most national sizzle—would be played on Sunday nights. CBS and FOX got the right to protect a certain number of games per year, generally moving those to the 4:25 PM ET slot. With TV ratings and TV dollars at an all-time high, great measures were taken to get the best games and best teams into the Sunday and Monday night slots.

Before 2019, the Browns played a Sunday night game in 2008. That was an early-season home loss to the Steelers, 10–6, and it dropped the Browns to 1–9 on *Sunday Night Football.* The lone win came on October 5, 2003, in Pittsburgh, 33–13. Through 2018, that still stood as the Browns' only win in Heinz Field, which opened in 2001.

77 Rolling Ball of Butcher Knives

Who's the best pro free agent signing of the Browns' new era? Phil Dawson doesn't count as he was basically still a rookie when the Browns acquired him. Jamir Miller had one big year, then never played again. Jeff Garcia and Robert Griffin III are easy scratches from the list.

A freak injury and subsequent staph infection kept LeCharles Bentley from ever playing a single down with the Browns. That same year, a big swing and miss on Kevin Shaffer led the Browns to drafting Joe Thomas the next year, and that worked out.

As for the best signing, Jamal Lewis is in the discussion. So, too, is Eric Steinbach, an athletic guard who helped clear paths for Lewis. If you notice a trend involving that 2007 offense, Joe Jurevicius delivered for the Browns, too, before an injury and staph infection cut his career short.

But as for consistency and long-term production, Orpheus Roye might be the best. A defensive end in a 3-4 defense in Pittsburgh, the Browns signed Roye in 2000 knowing he was

Orpheus Roye during a 2005 victory over the Titans. (Robert Skeoch/NFLPhotoLibrary/Getty Images)

versatile and athletic enough to play in any defense. He eventually played in multiple defenses for the Browns under three different coaches. The Browns gave Roye a $7.5 million signing bonus in 2000, but he actually took a pay cut two years later to stay with the team. That ended up being a win for the Browns.

Butch Davis once called Roye "a rolling ball of butcher knives," which was borrowed from the old-school football vernacular but pretty much fit. Roye could play inside and out. He was a solid interior pass-rusher and strong against the run regardless of scheme or position.

Roye played in 113 games for the Browns from 2000 to '07, which puts him just behind Dawson, Joe Thomas, and Joshua Cribbs among the new-era Browns. He had 9.5 sacks, three fumble recoveries, and two forced fumbles in his time with the Browns.

Roye had knee issues, which led to his release before the 2008 season. In a statement on his release, GM Phil Savage said Roye was "a mainstay for the Browns with his reliable play and overall dependability. He's a professional in every sense of the word."

Like Davis was with his rolling-ball-of-butcher-knives description, Savage was right.

78 The Big Blizzard Game

The Browns' magical 2007 season included the worst weather game of the first 20 years of the team's new era. On December 16, the Browns beat the Bills 8–0 as nearly a foot of snow fell on Downtown Cleveland. It was so bad that attempts by the grounds crew to clear off yard lines and hash marks were eventually abandoned.

Brady Quinn drops back to pass in a game in which the snow fell throughout and wind gusts reached 40 mph. (Scott Boehm/AP Photo)

It stands as one of the most memorable games of kicker Phil Dawson's long career. The Browns won, 8–0, on two Dawson field goals and a safety. Dawson opened the scoring with a 35-yarder, and his 49-yarder in the second quarter started 15 or 20 yards right before the wind gusts pushed it back towards the middle of the field and between the goal posts.

Former Ohio State star Dustin Fox became a Northeast Ohio media personality after his playing career, working for the Browns on their radio and TV networks. Fox was a backup safety for the Bills in 2008 and called the game in Cleveland "unforgettable" because of the elements.

"As a little kid you love to play in the snow. To do it in the NFL, it's pretty much a dream," Fox said. "The problem was there was so much snow it was miserable. You couldn't get footing. Your fingers and toes were numb. I'll never forget when Dawson came out for the long field goal. We couldn't believe they were actually trying it. It had to be a fake. It was a disaster out there.

"It's unbelievable that he made it. He was a maestro."

In Cleveland, the wind sometimes even gusts in the summer. In a December blizzard, it routinely gusts upwards of 40 MPH. So there was blowing snow in addition to standing snow.

"Sometimes you wouldn't even know the ball was in the air on a short pass unless you were right next to it," Fox said. "Eventually we just played every down like it was third and one. You pretty much couldn't throw, even if you wanted to."

The Bills attempted 33 passes because they played from behind most of the game, completing 13. Browns quarterback Derek Anderson was 9-of-24 passing for 137 yards. Jamal Lewis was built for that kind of game, and he carried 33 times for 163 yards as the Browns played keep-away.

Dawson is a native Texan, but he obsessed over the Cleveland weather to the point that he almost craved the challenge of a windy and snowy Sunday. During the week he'd stay in touch with the grounds crew about the wind direction and other weather issues. Watching the wind push that field goal back towards the uprights was all in the plans.

"Phil lived for those moments," punter and field-goal holder Dave Zastudil said. "He never doubted himself for a second."

79 Maneuvering for Wimbley

Browns GM Phil Savage made a trade with his friend and mentor, Ravens GM Ozzie Newsome, to start the 2006 Draft.

The Browns had the move in the works. They knew ESPN cameras would be on Haloti Ngata, so when the Browns were on the clock, Bill Rees, a top personnel lieutenant under Savage, called Ngata. The Ravens then saw Ngata on the phone, which the Browns believed would entice the Ravens to make the move.

Rees and Ngata made small talk. Rees joked with Ngata that he should smile because he was on TV. Meanwhile, Savage told Newsome that he should give a fourth-round pick to move up one spot, from No. 13 to No. 12, to keep the Browns from getting Ngata. They talked for several minutes before agreeing on a sixth-rounder, pick No. 181, which the Browns eventually used on Stanford defensive tackle Babatunde Oshinowo.

Oshinowo was not Ngata. And the player the Browns had long wanted, Kamerion Wimbley, was not Ngata either.

Savage had scouted the first game of Wimbley's final college season, and he'd said on and off the record that Wimbley had shown one pass-rush move in that game that was better than any move any of the Browns' 2005 pass-rushers had. Wimbley could bend around tackles and explode towards quarterbacks.

At the time, Savage, Romeo Crennel, and the Browns' other top decision-makers were on board with addressing the pass rush over taking Ngata or another interior defensive lineman. The Browns just hoped for more return, both from the trade and from Wimbley.

Wimbley had 11 sacks and three fumble recoveries as a rookie. He only missed one game in four seasons with the Browns, but his sack production tailed off as he totaled just nine sacks over his second and third seasons. After the 2009 season he was traded to the Raiders; that he was traded on the same day the Browns traded Brady Quinn says a lot about how the first 10 years of first-round picks for the new Browns went.

Wimbley played through 2014. He finished his career with 53.5 sacks, eight forced fumbles, and four fumble recoveries. Ngata became a star for the Ravens and an athletic force on a defense that was dominant in stretches.

Ngata retired after the 2018 season. He went to five Pro Bowls in nine years with the Ravens before playing with the Lions and Eagles to end his career.

80 Ohio State Pipeline

The old Browns' ties to Ohio State started with Paul Brown, who coached at Ohio State prior to World War II. He was the first Browns coach when the franchise began play in the AAFC in 1946 until 1962. Those Browns teams won four consecutive AAFC championships, then won NFL championships in 1950, 1954, and 1955.

Those early Browns teams had Ohio State players like Dante Lavelli, Tony Adamle, Bill Willis, Tommy James, and Lou Groza playing lead roles. Brown had coached at Ohio State from 1941 to '43 and was able to recruit those players to the new professional team. Though they drafted several players from Ohio State after joining the NFL in 1950, the Browns' first big draft hit from Ohio State was tackle Dick Schafrath in 1959. They selected linebacker Jim Houston in the first round the following season.

Through 2018, the 34 Ohio State players drafted by the Browns were the most from any school.

The Browns drafted end John Havlicek in 1962. The native of Bridgeport, Ohio, never played for the Browns but did okay for himself on the basketball floor, winning eight NBA championships while playing for the Boston Celtics. Two years later, the Browns struck gold with an Ohio-born pass-catcher out of Ohio State, Paul Warfield of Warren. Warfield was elected to the Pro Football Hall of Fame in 1983. He played in conference championship games with the Browns in each of his first five seasons.

An eight-time Pro Bowl pick, Warfield played six seasons for the Browns before being traded to the Dolphins in 1970, with whom he played on the unbeaten Super Bowl champions in 1972. He returned to the Browns for one season in 1976 and later worked for the new-era Browns in a high-level personnel executive role.

Before the Browns selected Denzel Ward at No. 4 overall in 2018—and Ward went to the Pro Bowl in his rookie season—the new-era Browns not drafting Ohio State players had angered many fans. Especially with Urban Meyer arriving at Ohio State in 2012 and bringing in top-tier talent from across the country, the Browns not drafting talented players who'd played college ball two hours down the highway was as puzzling as some of the players the Browns had taken during that time.

Darnell Sanders was a native of the Cleveland area. He was also average, at best, as an NFL tight end. A fourth-round pick in 2002, Sanders started 12 games in his second year and caught a touchdown pass in each of his two years with the Browns but never got a third. He played briefly with the Falcons after that and finished his career with 18 catches for 118 yards.

The Browns drafting Brian Robiskie in 2009 made for a wonderful hometown story. Though the son of NFL assistant coach Terry Robiskie had moved often as a child, he went to high school at Chagrin Falls in the Cleveland area and had served as a ballboy for the Browns in the summers when his father was on the staff of Butch Davis. Brian Robiskie was considered one of the top wide receiver prospects in the nation as a high schooler, and coming off an outstanding career at Ohio State the Browns selected Robiskie No. 36 overall.

Robiskie never made much of a splash in the NFL. The Browns didn't sign him until after training camp started, and he caught just seven passes as a rookie. He was much better in his second year, catching 29 passes and three for touchdowns, but the offense wasn't scaring anyone and Robiskie wasn't much of a deep threat. After playing in just six games in 2011, the Browns cut Robiskie. He then had short stints with the Lions and Falcons but was out of the league by 2014. He had 43 career receptions, four for touchdowns.

Ward became the first Ohio State defensive back drafted by the Browns since Dick LeBeau in 1959. LeBeau, also a native Ohioan, was cut by the Browns as a rookie. He caught on with the Lions, played six games as a rookie, and went on to have a Hall of Fame playing career before a lengthy and decorated coaching career.

Browns general manager John Dorsey, an avid football historian, was asked in early 2019 if the Ward pick might be the start of the Browns getting back to their old ways and regularly drafting players from Ohio State.

"Ohio State University puts out some very fine football players," Dorsey said. "We could go back to Bill Willis and Paul Warfield. There are some really good football players there. Any time you get a chance to acquire a really good football player, I'm all about that. I thought Denzel was a really quality football player and I think we're very lucky to have a guy like that on our team."

81 Hometown Hoyer

Brian Hoyer surprisingly went undrafted in 2009, but he landed with the Patriots as a backup and was able to hold that job for three years. When the Patriots cut him ahead of the 2012 season, Hoyer still believed he could one day play in the NFL if given the chance.

The Steelers signed him, then cut him. The Cardinals brought him aboard late in the season, calling him into injury duty, and then gave Hoyer a start in the 2012 season finale. But the following spring's free agency period came and went without Hoyer getting a contract. He was at home waiting for a call, and home was Cleveland.

In May 2013, the Browns called. Hoyer signed a two-year deal, but he was the third-string quarterback behind Brandon Weeden and Jason Campbell. The order pretty much stayed like that throughout the summer. There were no signs he'd end up with a 10–6 record as starting quarterback of the Browns, which by new-era Browns standards might as well have been 100–6.

But when Weeden got injured early in the season, the Browns turned to Hoyer over Campbell. Hoyer won his first game as the starter, and then the second. And the Browns were winning the third—a Thursday night home game with a raucous crowd—when Hoyer suffered a torn ACL just two drives in. His season was over. The Browns would go on to lose their last seven games to finish 4–12. One-year coach Rob Chudzinski got fired; a month or so later, top executives Joe Banner and Mike Lombardi did, too. The

Browns drafted Johnny Manziel, but Hoyer came back healthy and won a training camp competition, and he started the 2014 season as the Browns' quarterback.

His was an underdog story and a Cinderella story rolled into one. Hoyer grew up going to Browns games at Cleveland Municipal Stadium with his father, Axel. The Hoyers lived in North Olmsted, a western suburb not far from the Browns' day-to-day headquarters in Berea, and Brian Hoyer played at St. Ignatius High School in Cleveland.

A funny thing happened in that 2014 season. After a typically slow offensive start, the Browns got good. Hoyer wasn't being asked to do too much, but the Browns were running the ball well and Hoyer emerged as an on- and off-field leader. Offensive coordinator Kyle Shanahan and Hoyer were on the same page, and Hoyer threw just five interceptions in the first 10 games.

After the Browns won on Thursday night in Cincinnati in November 2014 to claim first place in the AFC North, Hoyer joined the NFL Network crew on set after the game. As he was interviewed, Browns fans still in the stadium chanted his name—loudly enough that eventually Hoyer acknowledged them. That sounds like something minor, but in the realm of the new Browns, that's sort of a landmark moment. The Browns went on the road and pushed around a divisional opponent. For a while, anyway, the Browns looked like they had a quarterback.

But Johnny Manziel was looming—GM Ray Farmer had been texting to the sidelines during games asking the Browns to play Manziel over Hoyer—and the 2014 season eventually went south. The Browns went from 7–4 to 7–9 with Hoyer getting benched, then hurt. Turnovers mounted, and a pass offense that looked to have been revitalized by the late November reinstatement of wide receiver Josh Gordon instead sunk with two struggling quarterbacks and lots of swirling drama.

Gordon didn't always run the right routes. Sometimes, Hoyer thought Gordon was barely running at all. Hoyer and Gordon had a physical confrontation following a practice late in that 2014 season. Hoyer knew the Browns were trying to replace him. Hoyer was not the type of guy to let a part-time player have his way.

After that 2014 season, Hoyer landed in Houston. He won the Texans' starting job in camp, then lost it to Ryan Mallett. The Texans later cut Mallett and turned back to Hoyer, who guided the Texans to the AFC South title. But the wildcard playoff game was a nightmare as Hoyer turned the ball over five times and the Chiefs rolled to victory. Two months later, the Texans signed Brock Osweiler and cut Hoyer.

Hoyer then landed in bad situations with both the Bears and 49ers, getting pressed into emergency duty for bad teams. After the 49ers landed Jimmy Garoppolo in a surprising 2017 trade, the Patriots suddenly had an opening for a backup quarterback and filled it with Hoyer once the 49ers cut him. Hoyer served as Tom Brady's primary backup for Super Bowl runs in both 2017 and 2018, and the Patriots won the Super Bowl following the 2018 season.

Through 11 NFL seasons, Hoyer had a 16–21 record as a starter and had made starts for five teams, but not the Patriots.

82 Bruce Arians, Still Angry

Bruce Arians has won a lot of games as an NFL head coach. He wanted to win some more with the Browns, and at least twice he campaigned for the Browns to hire him as head coach.

A longtime quarterback guru, Arians didn't get his first crack as an NFL head coach until he was 60. His first NFL offensive coordinator job was with the Browns in 2001, when he joined the staff of new coach Butch Davis and brought along the quarterback who started the first and, as of this writing, only playoff game of the Browns' new era, Kelly Holcomb.

Holcomb had been a backup in Indianapolis, where Arians served as quarterbacks coach from 1998 to 2000. Those were Peyton Manning's first three years in the NFL, and the stories of Manning's tireless work ethic include Manning wanting to take nearly every snap in practice. So Holcomb, an undrafted rookie with the Colts the year before Manning arrived, was largely an unknown commodity. But when Holcomb achieved free agent status in 2001, the Browns signed him to back up and serve as a mentor of sorts to Tim Couch, who followed Manning as the No. 1 overall pick in 1999. The Browns really ended up needing Holcomb in 2002.

Though Couch's best professional season was a big part of the 2002 Browns winning six road games and sneaking into the playoffs, Couch suffered a broken leg in the Browns' dramatic win over the Falcons in the regular-season finale. Holcomb played the final two-plus quarters of the Falcons game, his first action since that October. A 15-yard touchdown pass from Holcomb to Kevin Johnson against the Falcons gave the Browns the lead in the fourth quarter, and the Browns came out the next week in the wildcard round at Pittsburgh with a plan to let it fly.

Holcomb threw the ball 43 times in that wild and gut-wrenching Browns' loss, completing 26 of them for a franchise playoff record 429 yards. He threw three touchdowns and one interception, and if not for a fourth-quarter drop by Dennis Northcutt the Browns probably would have gone on to the next round in Oakland with a hot quarterback and aggressive play-caller. The defense just needed to make one more play in that game, too, and later Arians would call out Davis publicly for taking over the defensive play-calling and demanding the Browns play prevent defense while the Steelers rallied to win that game.

Fifteen years later, Arians was saying he was "still angry" about that game.

The Browns were so close, and though Holcomb started some games the next season when Couch was injured again, he never recaptured the magic of that early January day in Pittsburgh. Arians was fired by Davis after 2003. He caught on with the Steelers the next season, first serving as wide receivers coach then spending five years as offensive coordinator for teams that routinely beat up on the Browns. He was forced out of Pittsburgh by Mike Tomlin in 2011, then caught on with the Colts as offensive coordinator under Chuck Pagano, who'd also been an assistant on those Davis-led staffs with the Browns. When Pagano was diagnosed with leukemia during his first season on the job, Arians took over as interim head coach and was named NFL Coach of the Year for his work in helping the Colts to a 9–3 record and playoff berth in quarterback Andrew Luck's rookie season.

The Browns' job was open ahead of the 2013 season. The Haslam family had taken ownership, and there was at least some link there as Jimmy Haslam had previously owned a small part of the Steelers. But Arians said of the three times he was considered a legitimate head coaching candidate when the Browns had an opening—2009, 2011, and 2013—he only was contacted by the team once, in 2009, and never got an interview. Arians later told Cleveland-area reporters he had talked to the Browns in 2009 but found out that same day that the team had hired Eric Mangini.

Arians was hired by the Cardinals before the 2013 season. He had just one losing season in his time there and three times guided the Cardinals to double-digit victories. Though the NFL doesn't officially count his wins with the Colts since Pagano was technically the head coach, Arians' record as Colts' and Cardinals' head coach was 58–33–1. The most successful Browns' coach in the new era is Davis at 24–35. Romeo Crennel went 24–40.

"It just comes down to a quarterback," Arians said in 2015. "We're all tied to the quarterback. Some good coaches have come and gone. I really loved my time in Cleveland and I wish I would have had another opportunity."

After 2017, Arians stepped down for health reasons and said he was retired from coaching. In 2018, Arians was working as a game analyst for CBS Sports and openly campaigned for the Browns' job after Hue Jackson had been fired. On more than one occasion he called the Browns' job "the only one" he'd consider taking. Arians knows quarterbacks, and both on the air and in various interviews once the Browns' job was vacant he neither hid nor tempered his love for Baker Mayfield.

It's not known if the John Dorsey–led Browns and Arians ever formally discussed the opening, but Arians was apparently more willing to listen to other offers than he initially let on. He ended up getting hired by the Buccaneers while his close friend and former assistant Freddie Kitchens was hired by the Browns. Arians was offensive coordinator at the University of Alabama in the late 1990s when Kitchens played quarterback there. Kitchens had been on Arians' staff with the Cardinals in a variety of roles before joining the Browns as running backs coach and associate head coach in 2018, his springboard to eventually being named interim offensive coordinator and then head coach.

83 Baltimore Sting

The Browns' move to Baltimore was devastating for a fan base that had long been passionate about the Browns and had seen the team flirt with the Super Bowl at both ends of the 1980s.

That the Browns became the Baltimore Ravens was even more painful. Art Modell's backdoor deals did the unthinkable, shipping the team to Baltimore in 1996. Though Cleveland got to keep the colors and the Browns name, the Browns came back as an expansion team in 1999.

In their first draft as the Baltimore Ravens, the Ravens had two first-round picks. They selected Hall of Famers in offensive tackle Jonathan Ogden and linebacker Ray Lewis. In 2000, the Ravens won the Super Bowl. Ozzie Newsome, the Browns' all-time receiving leader, went with Modell to Baltimore as vice president of player personnel. He was named general manager in 2002 and kept that job through 2018, when he stepped aside but remained with the team. The Ravens won another Super Bowl in 2012.

The Browns had a chance to draft Ed Reed in 2002. Reed had played under then-Browns coach Butch Davis in college, but Davis selected running back William Green in the first round instead. Reed went on to a Hall of Fame career with the Ravens.

In 2005, the Browns hired Phil Savage as their general manager. Savage had long been Newsome's right-hand man in the Ravens' personnel department and had helped construct a team not just good enough to win the Super Bowl in 2000, but a defense that consistently was good enough to make the Ravens a playoff team.

Savage was aggressive in working to make the Browns a playoff-quality team, and in his third season the Browns went 10–6 and just missed the playoffs. His biggest mistakes were at the game's most important position. The Browns got one great season out of Derek Anderson—who, ironically, was claimed via waivers from the Ravens—but Anderson could not sustain that level of play.

Though Savage was fired after the Browns flopped in 2008 and he sent a regrettable email—it read: "F you, go root for Buffalo"—to a fan who had discovered his email address and voiced his displeasure, it was the miss with Brady Quinn in the 2007 Draft that probably really cost Savage and the Browns. Savage had hoped he'd get a chance to hire another head coach before 2009 and get the Browns back on track, but on the last day of the 2008 season, owner Randy Lerner fired both Savage and head coach Romeo Crennel a year after giving them contract extensions.

The Browns had traded their 2008 first-round pick to get back into the first round and draft the Ohio-born Quinn. But Quinn never became a quality starter for the Browns, who then spent more than a decade and several draft picks looking for one. As Savage debated making a move for Quinn during that 2007 Draft, he did so believing that Newsome and the Ravens might also be interested. The Ravens waited until the next year and drafted Joe Flacco, who won a Super Bowl in 2012 and didn't lose to the Browns until 2015.

While with the Ravens, Jamal Lewis had set an NFL record with 295 rushing yards against the Browns in 2003. Lewis later played for the Browns and became the only player in franchise history besides Jim Brown to run for 1,300 yards in a season. Savage also brought punter Dave Zastudil from the Ravens via free agency, but the Browns never were able to sustain the momentum they built in 2007 or create a dominant unit like the Ravens did defensively starting in the early 2000s.

Through 20 years of the series between the new Browns and the team that used to be the Browns, the Ravens held a 30–10 advantage. The Ravens were 19–3 vs. the Browns in Flacco's 11 seasons as quarterback.

84 Accidental Steelers Star

As if the 2004 season wasn't bad enough for the Browns on their own, they accidentally launched a Steelers linebacker to stardom.

If that sounds too crazy to be true, it's not. James Harrison was a journeyman special teams player who'd been cut by both the Steelers and Ravens before a training camp injury in 2004 gave Harrison one more shot to stick on the Steelers' active roster.

On November 14 of that season, the Steelers played in Cleveland. Before the game, Steelers starting outside linebacker Joey Porter and Browns running back William Green exchanged words. Green believed Porter had spit on him, and things escalated. They traded punches, and both were ejected before the game began, but *after* each team had submitted its list of inactive players.

Porter being out led to James Harrison getting his first NFL start, and the native of nearby Akron made the most of it. Harrison had a sack and six tackles as the Steelers won, proving to his coaches and teammates he could play at the game's highest level. By the end of that season he became a starter, and three years later he became a Super Bowl hero who signed a contract with the Steelers for more than $50 million.

Harrison would go on to become the 2008 NFL Defensive Player of the Year. He made five Pro Bowls before retiring after the 2017 with 84.5 career sacks.

Harrison's second most memorable day in Cleveland Browns Stadium might have come in 2005. With the Steelers blowing the Browns out on Christmas Eve, an inebriated fan ran onto the field and had gotten past the first wave of security. As the fan approached the Steelers' huddle, Harrison grabbed him and bodyslammed him to the turf, holding him there.

Later in his career, Harrison delivered three separate hits that gave Browns players Mohamed Massaquoi, Colt McCoy, and Joshua Cribbs concussions. Harrison was known for headhunting and frequently drew fines for his cheap shots. He didn't seem to care.

Cribbs was Harrison's college teammate for one season at Kent State. In a story that made the rounds when both became prominent NFL players, Cribbs was inserted into a scrimmage ahead of his freshman season. It was a full-speed, full-contact scrimmage except for quarterbacks, which Cribbs was at the time. After the upperclass quarterback took his reps, Cribbs went in and handed off in the direction opposite Harrison. On the next play, Cribbs ran the option to Harrison's side. He kept it, and as he turned upfield, Harrison planted him.

It was Cribbs' welcome-to-college moment, as the Browns later provided the NFL break Harrison needed.

85 Top Tight Ends

Six of the 10 top seasons in terms of receptions in franchise history have been posted by tight ends, starting with a three-way tie at the top.

Ozzie Newsome had 89 receptions in both 1983 and 1984. In 2006, Kellen Winslow Jr. had 89. Both were first-round picks and played significant roles in team history, albeit for different reasons.

Newsome was one of the greatest Browns and one of the greatest tight ends ever to play. Winslow Jr. was the son of one of the greatest tight ends ever to play, and one of the most disappointing players of the new Browns' era. Even in his two good seasons, the production never matched the potential—or the price the Browns paid for drafting Winslow instead of Ben Roethlisberger.

In the new era, two big receiving seasons by tight ends essentially came out of nowhere.

Both made their only Pro Bowl following their respective surprise seasons.

A fourth-round pick of the Tom Heckert/Mike Holmgren Browns in 2011, Jordan Cameron was originally a college basketball player who was relatively new to the game when the Browns drafted him. Heckert liked Cameron's raw athleticism and thought with proper work and seasoning, Cameron could turn into a weapon.

After the Browns submitted the pick, a public relations staffer dialed Cameron Jordan, a defensive end who'd been selected by the Saints in the first round. That conversation got a little awkward when Jordan told the staffer he wouldn't be joining Cleveland reporters for a conference call because he'd called the wrong person, and that story later got some traction among the hundreds of new-era Browns follies.

But after two years as a part-time player trying to find his way on a bad team, Cameron turned into a nice story in his own right. He got more comfortable and confident as he matured physically and learned, and in his third season he caught 80 passes, seven for touchdowns, and went to the Pro Bowl.

After four years in Cleveland, he played a season and a part of another with the Dolphins before concussions cut his career short.

Gary Barnidge had been a blocking tight end and a backup with the Panthers. He was signed by the Browns because then-coach Rob Chudzinski knew him well, and Chudzinski believed the Browns would benefit from Barnidge's experience and professionalism.

Before his big season, Barnidge never had more than 13 receptions in a single season. Near the end of that 2015 season, the Browns gave Barnidge an extension of three years for about $12 million, partly as a thank you for his contributions before he put up the big stats on a 3–13 team.

He started all 16 games again in 2016, catching 55 passes. He was cut in 2017 and chose not to play again.

Josh Gordon's 87 catches in 2013 and Kevin Johnson's 84 in 2001 round out the top five in team history. Winslow's second big season—when he had 82, scored five touchdowns, and went to his only Pro Bowl in 2007—ranks sixth.

86 Gary Baxter's Devastating Injury

Gary Baxter could play all over the secondary, and heading into 2005 the Browns needed playmakers. But Baxter's injury issues ended up making him one of the biggest free-agent busts of the team's new era, and the injury that ended his career goes down as one of the most bizarre in NFL history.

While defending a deep pass in a 2006 game vs. the Broncos, Baxter ended up tearing the patella tendons in both of his knees. It's believed he became just the second player in NFL history to suffer the major injury in both knees, and though he attempted a comeback it never worked out.

Baxter made it back to the practice field in 2007 and vowed he'd get back to the starting lineup. The Browns let Baxter back in practice on a limited basis and fully supported his comeback attempt, but he ended up going on injured reserve in 2007. He was released in 2008.

When Phil Savage joined the Browns as general manager in 2005, he signed Baxter because he was familiar with the tall defensive back's skill set and believed Baxter would provide savvy and leadership for the Browns' defense. Savage came to the Browns from the Ravens, who had selected Baxter in the second round in 2002.

Baxter signed a six-year deal worth $30 million and got $10.5 million as a signing bonus. He suffered a torn pectoral muscle five games into his first season with the Browns and ended up playing in just eight games over two years with the Browns. He had two interceptions in 2005 and one in 2006 before the double injury.

While playing with the Ravens in 2004, Baxter delivered a hit that injured Steelers quarterback Tommy Maddox and forced rookie quarterback Ben Roethlisberger to come in. Fifteen years later, Roethlisbeger was still the Steelers' quarterback and the rest was a rather dark part of the Browns' history.

Baxter played mostly safety with the Ravens but also had played cornerback, which was his primary position with the Browns. His injury led the Browns to draft two cornerbacks in 2007, Eric Wright in the second round and Brandon McDonald in the fifth.

87 Freddie Kitchens

Freddie Kitchens didn't take the fast track. He started his coaching career the first year the Browns returned to the NFL as a low-level assistant in Glenville, West Virginia, at Division II Glenville State.

But he took the fast track with the Browns. After being hired as running backs coach and assistant head coach in January 2018, he was promoted to offensive coordinator at the end of October following the firings of head coach Hue Jackson and offensive coordinator Todd Haley. Kitchens had never been a play-caller before, but he was good enough with rookie quarterback Baker Mayfield that in January 2019, the Browns named Kitchens their full-time head coach.

He'd never done that before, either. The Browns won five of their last seven games in 2018 but never really considered keeping

Baker Mayfield talks to then–offensive coordinator Freddie Kitchens during the Browns' Week 13 game against the Texans. (Kevin Terrell/AP Photo)

interim coach Gregg Williams. They formally interviewed seven candidates and intentionally saved Kitchens for last.

On January 9, 2019, John Dorsey informed Kitchens that he was going to be named the 17th head coach in franchise history, the ninth in the team's new era.

"Freddie has dedicated his entire life to the game of football," Dorsey said. "He has been around some exceptional football guys. He is a real unifier of men and people. Freddie did an outstanding job the last eight games of the [2018] season. He galvanized the offense, he put players in positions to make plays and Freddie has a great vision for this organization moving forward."

A quarterback at Alabama, Kitchens was selling cars and washing trucks in Tuscaloosa once his playing career ended. But his heart was in football, and he landed a grad assistant job under Nick Saban at LSU after his stint at Glenville State. From there he worked at North Texas and Mississippi State before catching on with the Dallas Cowboys in 2006.

Kitchens then went to the Arizona Cardinals, working under head coach Ken Whisenhunt and Haley. Kitchens stayed with the Cardinals when Bruce Arians was hired as head coach in 2012. A former Browns offensive coordinator, Arians was offensive coordinator at the University of Alabama for Kitchens' final college season.

Kitchens had been on Arians' staff with the Cardinals in a variety of roles before joining the Browns, where he'd been recruited by Haley. They first worked together on the Cowboys' staff in 2006, then Kitchens replaced Haley in the middle of the 2018 season.

By 2019, the Browns had the maximum number of national TV games. Outside expectations were sky-high with Kitchens calling the plays, Mayfield in his second year and the Browns having acquired all-everything wide receiver Odell Beckham Jr. in a trade. But Kitchens insisted that he welcomed high expectations and was looking forward to—finally—being the coach who got things right.

"Since 1999, there have been ups and downs in this organization," Kitchens said at his introductory press conference. "Since 1999, I understand and I relish the fact that there have been more downs than ups, but that ends today. I promise you that. Every decision we make as an organization—and John would agree with this, I am sure he would—every decision will be based on one thing and one thing only, that is winning football games.

"Let's not fool ourselves, this game is about winning. Everything that we do in the organization from the football side of things moving forward, with the organization moving forward—if you do not wear Brown and Orange, you do not matter. The only organization that we care anything about right now is the Cleveland Browns. It is always going to be about one thing and one thing only and that is about winning football games and putting a good product on the field that plays with effort, enthusiasm, and toughness."

88 Are You a Coach?

With the Browns entering a second season of being the league's youngest team in 2017 and having drafted three players in the first round—none over 21—some of the team's decision makers decided it would be a good idea to start the annual rookie minicamp by inviting some past players to dinner with the rookies and coaches.

Joe Thomas, who was entering his 11th NFL season at the time, was also invited. Hall of Famer Jim Brown addressed the group about opportunities and expectations. Several other former players talked about the team's rich tradition and what it would mean to the city for the Browns to get back to winning. Thomas was mostly hanging out, introducing himself to his new teammates, and things got a little awkward when first-round tight end David Njoku first talked with Thomas.

Njoku had a specific question, so he asked Thomas if he was a coach.

Thomas couldn't quit laughing. He assured Njoku that although he was balding and might look older than he actually was, he was still on the team.

Rookie minicamp weekends are always a little hectic. Though the draft picks get preferential treatment, they have to fill out much of the same paperwork and go through the same tedious processes as the undrafted rookies and tryout players do. In most cases, the rookies are inside the building for the first time. So awkward moments happen all the time. Thomas just happened to share this one with the outside world.

Thomas tweeted about Njoku's question, and the rookie later admitted to being embarrassed about it.

"I just hope Joe will forgive me," Njoku said.

They'd end up being teammates for half a season. A little more than a month after playing his 10,000th consecutive snap, Thomas suffered a torn triceps in an October home game vs. the Titans and left the field for the first time in his Hall of Fame career. He formally announced his retirement after the season.

The Browns traded back into that 2017 first round to get Njoku knowing that he'd need time to develop. He wasn't a full-time player in college, and even after a breakout sophomore season at the University of Miami his decision to enter the NFL was not an easy one. But Njoku has a rare combination of size and speed, and though parts of the game will likely never come easy to him, he's a big target and is difficult to take down after the catch. Once Baker Mayfield and the Browns got rolling in the back half of the 2018 season, Njoku started to play with more confidence and become a more consistent producer.

89 A Double Miss in 2012

Heading into the 2012 Draft, the Browns had an all-too-familiar problem. They needed a quarterback.

But there were other issues. Sitting at pick No. 4 after another awful season, they clearly needed help at other positions, too. And with quarterbacks all but a lock to go in the first two spots, the Browns couldn't get their first choice and didn't love any of their other choices.

The Browns weren't getting the rights to the No. 1 pick and Andrew Luck from the Colts, despite Mike Holmgren making a godfather offer. The Colts were cutting Peyton Manning and saw Luck as a generational prospect. The Browns could have kept offering more picks and the Colts wouldn't have budged. Any discussions they had with the Rams about moving up to No. 2 never materialized, and the Rams ended up making a trade with Washington that allowed the Redskins to move up and select Robert Griffin III at No. 2. Eventually, just minutes before the draft began, the Browns negotiated a trade of one spot with the Vikings, who allowed the Browns to move up to No. 3 and select running back Trent Richardson of Alabama.

Richardson was powerful, fast, and had the look of a workhorse back. He got off to a solid start, too, setting new franchise rookie records with 950 rushing yards and 11 rushing touchdowns in 2012. But that trade ended up being the first of two awful trades involving Richardson, who played just three NFL seasons and in just 17 games with the Browns. Too strong for many college defenders to tackle and the lead back on a loaded Alabama team, Richardson was ordinary by NFL standards. The NFL had fully

Playoff Tickets?

Mike Holmgren's stint running the Browns was short and unsuccessful. Owner Randy Lerner wanted Holmgren to coach the team, but Holmgren understandably liked his role as team president at a reported $8 million per year.

Under Holmgren and his hand-picked general manager, Tom Heckert, the Browns drafted two quarterbacks, Colt McCoy and Brandon Weeden. Holmgren had made his name in the NFL as a developer of quarterbacks such as Brett Favre and Matt Hasselbeck, but there would be no such success story in his three years with the Browns.

In a December 2011 press conference after the Browns and Holmgren's hand-picked head coach, Pat Shurmur, had allowed McCoy to return to a game after suffering a concussion, Holmgren got particularly defensive. The Browns were headed to another losing season, and Holmgren took exception to some of the questioning.

"It seems as though it's business as usual, which is very easy to write and say," Holmgren said. "But I'm telling you, it is not. And you can choose to believe me or you can say, 'Nah, I've heard it before.' That's your choice. But when it does happen, don't come to me for extra tickets for a playoff game or something. You're either with us or you're not. And I'll be honest with you, sometimes I feel, not everybody... no I won't. I'm telling you, it's different now."

It was not different, and the Holmgren experiment didn't last long. Lerner sold the team the following summer to Jimmy and Dee Haslam. The Browns went 5–11 in each of Shurmur's two years as head coach, and Holmgren was out shortly after the Haslams officially took over in October 2012.

In the end, no one had to call Holmgren for playoff tickets.

become a quarterback-driven league, and the Browns traded to No. 3 to select a running back who totaled 17 career touchdowns.

In quarterback desperation, they'd later reach for 28-year-old Brandon Weeden at pick No. 22.

In the draft-night trade, the Vikings slid one spot back and took USC tackle Matt Kalil, the player they were probably taking anyway. The Browns also gave up picks in the fourth, fifth, and seventh rounds of the 2012 Draft. In retrospect, the Browns got swindled by the Vikings in trading up just one spot. But the Browns had a bunch of picks and clearly weren't hitting home runs with them. They had a left tackle in place and dodged a bullet by not taking Oklahoma State wide receiver Justin Blackmon, who went No. 5 to the Jaguars and saw his career get derailed by off-field issues. Beyond Luck, there wasn't another home run pick in that draft until the Panthers took linebacker Luke Kuechly at No. 9.

As a rookie, Richardson ran well—and usually with confidence—for a bad team. Despite playing much of the season with a broken rib, he rarely shied away from contact and only missed one game.

But the 2012 season marked the ownership change, with the Haslam family taking over and Joe Banner and Mike Lombardi taking over the football side before the 2013 season. Holmgren, then-coach Pat Shurmur, and general manager Tom Heckert were all fired. Rob Chudzinski was hired as head coach and brought along the pass-happy Norv Turner as offensive coordinator. Richardson didn't make a strong first impression with the new group. He struggled to see holes opening in front of him and had just 105 rushing yards on 31 attempts in the first two games of 2013.

When the Colts offered a first-round pick in hopes Richardson would become the kind of bell-cow back who could support Luck and keep defenses honest, the Browns had no choice but to trade him for the Colts' 2014 first-round pick. The Browns knew they weren't winning anything of consequence until they got a quarterback, and by early in 2013 they knew Weeden wasn't that quarterback. That was problematic for several reasons, primarily that the Browns had used their second first-round pick a few hours after they'd drafted Richardson to select Weeden at No. 22 overall. Neither made it to a third season with the Browns.

The Colts got three rushing touchdowns out of Richardson in 2013, but he never emerged as their lead back. In two playoff games in 2013 he got four carries for a total of one yard. Richardson scored three touchdowns for the Colts in 2014 but was cut in March 2015. He went to camp with the Raiders in 2015 but was released before the regular season began. He got a chance with the Ravens in 2016 but injuries prevented him from ever making it to the field, then he played in four games in 2017 for the Saskatchewan Roughriders of the Canadian Football League. Richardson did not show up for training camp with the Roughriders the following year, forcing the team to put him on the suspended list before ultimately releasing him.

He was last seen playing for the Birmingham Iron in the Alliance of American Football, a new league that launched—and folded—in early 2019.

90 Heinz Mirage

Nine months after losing a 17-point lead and losing in Heinz Field in a wildcard playoff game following the 2002 season, the 2003 Browns went back to Heinz Field and pushed the Steelers around in a nationally televised Sunday night game. The Browns had entered that game at 1–3, but Tim Couch was back from injury and that performance gave off vibes that the Browns were getting things right and preparing to make another run.

Beating the Steelers will do that. This wasn't exactly Joe "Turkey" Jones dumping Terry Bradshaw on his head, as the Browns' defensive end did in 1976. This wasn't the 1989 Browns opening the season by beating the Steelers, 51–0, in Pittsburgh. But at the time it felt like a turning point.

It wasn't. Through 18 seasons of the Steelers playing in Heinz Field, it still stands as the Browns' only win there. And what might have been Couch's best win ended up coming in his last game against the Steelers.

Couch threw two touchdown passes and was 20-of-25 for 208 yards. The Browns didn't have to throw much over the final 30 minutes, and William Green ground out 115 rushing yards on 33 carries in front of what became a silent and empty crowd in the final quarter.

Daylon McCutcheon, one of the rare solid yet underrated draft picks of the team's new era, returned an interception 75 yards for a touchdown early in the third quarter as the Browns made it 30–10 and turned it into a laugher.

Things turned bad soon after. Two weeks after the win in Pittsburgh, Green was suspended for violating the league's substance abuse policy. During that suspension, he was arrested for DUI.

Couch started just six more games, winning two, as he dealt with elbow and shoulder issues. The Browns wanted him to take a pay cut after the season and weren't sure he would get healthy enough to be in their plans. After signing Jeff Garcia in March 2004, the Browns cut Couch.

Though he caught on briefly with the Packers, the elbow issues basically ended his career. Couch had suffered a broken leg in the 2002 season finale after posting his best season and didn't play in that playoff game. He'd missed the first two games of 2003 and later missed four more games. With his completion percentage falling short of 50 percent over the last three games of 2003 and the Browns finishing 5–11, Davis felt pressure mounting and couldn't wait on Couch.

Couch started 59 of 62 games for the Browns, playing in a full season just once. He completed 60 percent of his passes, throwing 64 touchdowns and 67 interceptions. He completed two Hail Mary passes to win games, but perhaps just as memorably he was sacked 166 times in those 62 games.

"There were good moments," Couch said in 2018. "I'm more frustrated because I didn't play up to my potential consistently. There were glimpses of it, certainly, games I really played good football. There were times and stretches, and then I would take a step back or get an injury.

"In 2002 I thought I was playing my best and I thought we were really building something. But I broke my leg and that really changed the whole projection of my career.

"I didn't get to play [in the playoff game] and then there's a quarterback controversy [with Kelly Holcomb] and I just never recovered from it. I just felt where I started with this team to where we were, I thought we were totally on the right track. I just couldn't stay healthy enough to do it consistently. That part, really, I've never been able to get over."

91 Teaming Up

In 1985, Kevin Mack and Earnest Byner became just the third duo in NFL history to each go over 1,000 rushing yards in the same season. Mack ran for 1,104 and went to the Pro Bowl in his first NFL season. Byner got 1,002 and also had 460 receiving yards.

Byner went on to have two different stints with the Browns in his 14-year career that included three 1,000-yard seasons, two Pro Bowl appearances, and 56 rushing touchdowns. But he's most remembered in Cleveland for The Fumble in Denver in the AFC Championship Game following the 1987 season.

Jim Brown led the NFL in rushing eight times. His dominance didn't leave many carries for other players, but he had pretty good running mates. The Browns used Bobby Mitchell as a wingback, receiver, and occasional sub for Brown, and he scored 32 total touchdowns in four seasons before finishing his Hall of Fame career with the Redskins.

The Browns drafted Leroy Kelly in 1964. He didn't play much in his first two seasons but led the NFL in rushing touchdowns in each of the first three seasons following Brown's retirement in 1965. Ernie Green had 15 rushing touchdowns from 1964 to '67, when he was a fullback for Brown and Kelly.

Mike and Greg Pruitt (no relation) made for a pretty good combo in the 1970s. Greg Pruitt went to four Pro Bowls in his time with the Browns from 1973 to 1981 and had three 1,000-yard seasons. Mike Pruitt scored 47 rushing touchdowns for the Browns from 1976 to 1984. He was a smaller back—he insists he hid a five-pound weight under a towel the first time a Browns' scout weighed him so he'd be over 170 pounds—and later became a weapon in the passing game.

Through 2018, there had been 23 1,000-yard rushing seasons in team history. Fourteen of them were by someone with the last name Pruitt or Brown.

Greg Pruitt's 65 receptions in 1981 are the most by a running back in team history. Eric Metcalf is next with 63 in 1993. Metcalf was the Greg Pruitt of the late 1980s and early 1990s. He got almost 200 touches for the 1993 Browns, accounting for more than 1,100 offensive yards in a season that featured his signature game. Metcalf had two punt return touchdowns.

Metcalf ran for a career-best 633 yards and six touchdowns as a rookie in 1989. He totaled just six more rushing touchdowns over the rest of his career but remained a dynamic returner and productive pass-catching back. He had at least 47 receptions in five of his six seasons with the Browns. Mack and Leroy Hoard, another big back, did much of the heavy lifting with Metcalf serving as a scatback and pass-catcher out of the backfield.

92 McCarron Trade

At the midpoint of the infamous 0–16 season, things started to get really ugly. The Browns lost in London to slip to 0–8, and after the game Hue Jackson publicly took on Sashi Brown and the personnel department. After getting blown out by the Vikings in a game they led at halftime, Jackson essentially told reporters that the Browns were so talent-deficient that their only hope to win was to play the perfect game.

And the perfect game, Jackson said, was not attainable.

The Browns flew home that night, about 36 hours before the trade deadline. And at some point between Sunday night and late

Tuesday morning, Jackson decided he wanted A.J. McCarron to be the quarterback.

Jackson was right that the Browns were going nowhere fast with overmatched rookie DeShone Kizer. He'd tried Kevin Hogan in place of Kizer for one game, and Hogan was worse. Jackson just wanted to win—both to try to save his job and to avoid 0–16 infamy—and he believed McCarron would be a better option.

Jackson had coached McCarron when Jackson was the offensive coordinator of the Bengals. In his only real NFL action to that point, McCarron had taken over in December for an injured Andy Dalton and played well enough to help the Bengals keep their grip on the AFC North. McCarron and the Bengals should have won a home playoff game against the Steelers but collapsed late in a head-scratching loss after longtime problem children Adam Jones and Vontaze Burfict picked up late penalties.

McCarron was available in 2017 because the Bengals were committed to Dalton. McCarron's exact free agency status at that time was still uncertain based on his not playing as a rookie, but the Bengals thought they'd lose him for nothing at the end of the season—and didn't see that as a devastating loss.

Old grudges die hard, though, and Bengals owner Mike Brown wasn't sure he wanted to deal with the Browns. The son of Hall of Fame coach and first coach of the Browns Paul Brown, Mike Brown never forgave Art Modell for firing his father and had vowed never to trade with the Browns.

But as negotiations progressed, Brown was willing to trade McCarron for second and third-round picks. He told his confidants he would not budge from that as the asking price and that the Browns could call back with a final answer, not an amended offer. The Bengals knew they'd be robbing the Browns in the deal, which is the only reason Mike Brown was willing to make it.

After several calls, the Browns said they would do the deal. The Bengals sent the paperwork, but the Browns did not submit it to the league office by the 4:00 PM deadline. Jackson was obviously working with permission of ownership to get McCarron, but Sashi Brown wasn't on board. So whether by sabotage, accident, or just poor timing—probably the first, but possibly a combination of the three—the trade was disallowed because paperwork was not submitted by the deadline.

Around the league and around the country, the Browns were getting laughed at, again.

Five months later, McCarron was granted unrestricted free agency but had few suitors. He signed with the Bills for two years and $10 million but was beaten out in camp by rookie Josh Allen and second-year player Nathan Peterman. The Bills then traded McCarron to the Raiders, where he spent the season serving as Derek Carr's backup. The Browns ended up using their own second-round pick on offensive lineman Austin Corbett and trading their third-round pick to Buffalo for Tyrod Taylor, who became their stopgap quarterback.

So, Sashi Brown's lasting legacy with the Browns isn't just the hoarding of draft picks. It's saving those two—and saving the team from what would have been a terrible trade by any measure.

McCarron would later say he was disappointed that the trade didn't go through and that he believed he could have gotten his career on track with the Browns. Jackson was so desperate for one win on the field and a win in what was becoming an ugly power struggle behind the scenes that he was willing to dump two picks for a player with three career starts.

"I got a call [around 3:30] from my agent telling me to stay by the phone. The next call I got was at 4:03 and [my agent said] 'Hey, the trade didn't go through. They didn't get the paperwork in on time,'" McCarron said in a radio interview a few months after the trade that wasn't. "Everybody has a story. I'm sure Cleveland has their own story, Cincy has their own story. But it's just one of those things, when you think you've seen everything, you're shown a little bit more. I think the only people who truly know what happened were the ones leading the whole situation on both sides."

It was clear then that the Brown-Jackson combination atop the Browns' organizational chart wasn't going to last. Jackson won out as Brown was fired five weeks after the trade deadline. Jackson returned for a third season but only made it halfway through. In 2019, McCarron was a backup with the Texans. Neither Sashi Brown nor Jackson was working in the NFL.

93 Center for One Snap

LeCharles Bentley was a mauler. He had violent hands and a desire not just to move opposing defensive linemen and linebackers, but to punish them.

At the start of free agency in 2006, Bentley signed a six-year, $36 million contract to play center for his hometown team. He never played a down for the Browns.

On the first play of the full training camp practice that summer, Bentley briefly engaged nose tackle Ted Washington. Bentley crumbled to the ground shortly thereafter, grabbing at his left knee. He suffered a torn patellar tendon, and Bentley cried on the practice field knowing his season was over.

Bentley would later acquire a staph infection while doing rehab work in the team's Berea facility. The infection became so severe that Bentley had to be hospitalized, and he'd later say at one point he believed he was going to die. Doctors at one point told him they'd worried that his left leg may need to be amputated.

He briefly attempted a comeback in 2008 after passing a physical but never made it back to the field. In 2012, Bentley and then-owner Randy Lerner worked out a deal to settle a lawsuit Bentley had filed in 2010 related to his staph infection.

Bentley grew up in Cleveland, starring at St. Ignatius High School before playing at Ohio State. He was a two-time Pro Bowl pick in his four seasons with the Saints. Headed into that offseason, general manager Phil Savage had targeted Bentley, punter Dave Zastudil (Bay High School/Ohio University), and wide receiver Joe Jurevicius (Mentor Lake Catholic High School) not just because they were good players, but because of their Ohio roots. Savage knew Browns fans were anxious to root for a winner again, and he felt those players could solve what Savage felt was a disconnect between the fan base and the new organization.

The Browns also signed veteran linebacker Willie McGinest in that free agent class, a sign that the team was serious about winning. McGinest was a two-time Pro Bowl pick and a three-time Super Bowl winner with the Patriots. He remains the NFL's all-time post-season sack leader and played three years with the Browns.

The Browns got decent return out of the rest of their 2006 free agent class. Zastudil became one of the league's best punters, while Jurevicius had one of his best seasons as part of the high-flying 2007 offense. But before the next season Jurevicius also got a staph infection, ending his career. He also settled a lawsuit out of court with the Browns.

Washington's best days were behind him, but the mammoth nose tackle made sense for the Browns in 2006 because he knew Romeo Crennel's defense. He was a starter for two seasons.

Kevin Shaffer didn't live up to his big contract, but he slid over to right tackle the following year when the Browns drafted Joe Thomas. He started 47 games in three seasons with the Browns.

The circumstances of Bentley's injury and botched recovery were part of a dark period for the new Browns, one from which the organization spent more than a decade trying to recover.

94 Ty's Time was Short

Ty Detmer started the first game for the new Browns. That's often forgotten for several reasons, starting with most Browns fans wanting to forget that 43–0 loss. Tim Couch finished that game, and the top pick of the new era was made the starter the following week.

Detmer was a Heisman Trophy winner who was mostly a backup during his NFL career. The Browns worked out a contract and traded for him ahead of the 1999 season because they thought he'd make a great tutor for the rookie they eventually picked. It took all of one game for a 20-year trend of impatience to begin.

Detmer started again in the 1999 season finale after Couch was injured. His numbers weren't great but he kept the Browns in the game in what became a wild 29–28 loss to the Colts.

Detmer tore his Achilles tendon in a 2000 preseason game and sat out the whole season. At the end of the 2001 preseason, he was traded to the Lions for draft picks. And three weeks later, he participated in a bit of Browns history.

On September 23, 2001, the Browns tied a franchise record with seven interceptions in a 24–14 home win over the Lions. Detmer threw all seven of them, and Browns rookie cornerback Anthony Henry had three interceptions.

Detmer finished 22-of-42 for 212 yards. He was sacked three times in addition to the interceptions. In addition to Henry's three interceptions, Detmer was also intercepted by Jamir Miller, Percy Ellsworth, Earl Little, and Corey Fuller.

It was just an ugly game. There were 24 accepted penalties, 15 for 115 yards on the Lions. The teams combined to convert just

3-of-23 third down chances. Neither team got 200 passing yards; the Browns only had 118. But the interceptions set up short fields, and the Browns cashed in. Their second touchdown came on a tackle-eligible play to extra offensive lineman Shaun O'Hara.

The seven interceptions tied the franchise record for most in a game previously set on December 11, 1960, as the Browns handed the Chicago Bears their worst defeat, 42–0. Bobby Franklin had three interceptions in that game, and Jim Shofner—who would later be interim head coach of the Browns in 1990—had two interceptions.

Henry was a darn good fourth-round pick. He would go on to finish his rookie season with 10 interceptions. He had another three-interception game as a rookie, in a Week 10 win over the Ravens. He also set franchise records that year with a 97-yard interception return touchdown in the infamous Bottlegate game vs. the Jaguars and with 177 total interception return yards on the season.

95 The Great Lakes Classic

NFL teams used to set their own preseason schedules—mostly, anyway—and in 2002, Browns CEO Carmen Policy called Lions president Matt Millen and wanted not just to establish a preseason rivalry of sorts, but to up the ante.

And so the Great Lakes Classic was born. Before the Lions and Browns went through periods of historic losing, they were traditionally strong franchises located about a three-hour drive apart. With both sitting next to Great Lakes, Policy thought using the lake theme and establishing a trophy (even though both teams had one) would be a good way to bring the game some attention. Each

Barkevious Mingo stands with Commissioner Goodell after being selected sixth overall by the Browns on April 25, 2013, at Radio City Music Hall in New York. (Gregory Payan/AP Photo)

team picked a preferred charity, with the winning team's choice getting around $30,000 each year, and the sides feigned a rivalry. Kind of.

It was so cheesy that sports radio callers and internet commenters adopted the Great Lakes Classic as sort of a mock rallying cry through the years when the Browns struggled. Both teams had received giant bronze barge trophies when the idea was born, and some fans would jokingly say that they hoped the Browns could at least bring home the barge.

This is not meant to demean Policy. He was a highly successful and respected executive. He knew the league, he knew the league's heaviest hitters and he worked hard to establish the Browns as more than an expansion team. If anything, he was probably having fun with the concept, though he did ask Browns' staffers to explore if there was a way to travel by water between Cleveland and Detroit.

The Great Lakes Classic idea was a spinoff of something the 49ers had done when Policy worked there. To add spice to an otherwise drab preseason, the 49ers and Broncos established a Rocky Mountain Challenge, complete with a trophy and the pledge to donate to the winning team's charity. The Great Lakes Classic went away for a while but returned in 2018, and No. 1 pick Baker Mayfield started and led the Browns to a win.

In 2005, the visiting Browns won the Great Lakes Classic when Charlie Frye threw the winning touchdown to Braylon Edwards, a Detroit native. That was exciting in the moment because both were rookies and the Browns were trying to create some positive energy.

That the Browns brought home The Barge made it even more special.

96 The 2013 Draft

Unlike those just before and after it, the 2013 Draft didn't have a swing and a miss at quarterback. But it basically had nothing but misses.

By 2016, the Browns had no players from that class still on the team. Add that to the 2012 Draft starting with Trent Richardson and Brandon Weeden and the 2014 Draft starting with Justin Gilbert and Johnny Manziel, and the stage was set for a period of historic losing from 2015 to '17.

The 2013 Draft was the only one with Joe Banner and his hand-picked general manager, Mike Lombardi, in charge. Banner was running the show, and he knew it was not a strong draft class. Banner ended up trading away the Browns' fourth and fifth-round picks in 2013 for 2014 picks, which wasn't a bad strategy. But starting the draft with outside linebacker Barkevious Mingo in the first round at No. 6 overall and then picking cornerback Leon McFadden in the third round, at pick No. 68 was a very bad strategy.

The *St. Louis Post-Dispatch* reported that the Rams, wanting to trade up to select speedy wide receiver Tavon Austin offered the Browns pick No. 16, a second-round pick and a seventh-round pick to move up to No. 6. Whether the Browns didn't want to lose Mingo or just didn't want to make more picks, they stuck with Mingo. And he barely became a starting-level player.

The Browns didn't have a second-round pick in 2013 because they'd spent it in the previous summer's Supplemental Draft on a talented but troubled wide receiver named Josh Gordon. With Gordon, the flashes of brilliance never outweighed the long-term headaches.

The issue with Mingo is there weren't enough flashes. He had burst off the edge, but he wasn't strong enough to be an every-down player. The Browns got seven sacks out of Mingo in three seasons before trading him in 2016 to the Patriots for a future fifth-round pick.

McFadden played just one year for the Browns. He started two games but recorded no interceptions or pass breakups. He bounced around the league in the years that followed.

After the trades, the Browns selected Notre Dame safety Jamoris Slaughter in the sixth round.

Slaughter had suffered a ruptured Achilles tendon in his final college season at Notre Dame. He'd been a good player before the injury and a full-time starter for two seasons, but the injury cost him a chunk of his final season and kept him from participating in the physical parts of the pre-draft process.

On a conference call not long after being picked, Slaughter told Cleveland-area reporters he was surprised that he was drafted. He never made it. Slaughter got back on the field but was cut at the end of his first training camp, then spent his rookie season on the practice squad. The Browns cut him in the summer of 2014.

The Browns took players from Division II colleges in the seventh round, defensive end Armonty Bryant and offensive guard Garrett Gilkey. Bryant recorded 8.5 sacks in three seasons with the Browns but was cut after getting arrested on drug charges on Christmas morning 2015.

Bryant was talented enough that the Lions gave him a chance after the Browns cut him. He served a suspension and then played in five games for the Lions in 2016, recording three sacks and a forced fumble. But he never played another NFL snap after that.

Gilkey played one season with the Browns, making one emergency start at left guard and otherwise playing as a backup and on special teams. He was cut before his second season and then played one season in a similar role for the Buccaneers.

The Browns got a total of 99 games and 23 starts out of their 2013 draft class. Bryant had more sacks (8.5) in his three seasons with the Browns than Mingo (7) did in his three seasons. McFadden lasted just one season with the team.

Compounding the issue with the 2013 Draft was that outside of getting an immediate starter at right tackle in Mitchell Schwartz, the Browns didn't get much from their 2012 Draft, either. Richardson had a strong rookie season, then was traded two games into his second season. The Weeden pick was pretty clearly a reach from early on in his rookie season.

Defensive tackle John Hughes became a solid interior player, and Travis Benjamin added some pop to the return game once the Browns moved on from Joshua Cribbs. But trading down to let the Falcons have Julio Jones was a move made with the intention of securing extra picks to help the Browns accelerate their rebuilding process. Instead, that 2012 Draft became another in an all-too-long line of drafts that set the Browns back—and the 2013 Draft became one of the worst of them all.

97 The Bottles Were Flying

The old Dawg Pound at Cleveland Municipal Stadium was legendary. And notorious. The stories of flying objects and outrageous behavior get better (and harder to believe) with age, but the fact is a 1989 game was stopped and the Broncos were permitted to go to the other end because of what Browns fans were throwing at them.

In the new era, the Dawg Pound was a little fancier but still designed to be for the rowdiest fans. Eventually, both common sense and heightened security measures made it almost nothing like the old experience. But, predictably, the new Dawg Pound had its infamous moment in 2001.

Down 15–10 to the Jaguars in the final minute of a December game, the Browns were driving towards the Dawg Pound end. After starting at their own 34-yard line, they'd moved the ball inside the Jaguars' 20-yard line. On fourth-and-2 at the 12, Tim Couch jammed the ball through traffic to a diving Quincy Morgan for what appeared to be a game-extending first down, and the Browns hustled to the line to run their first-down play with the clock ticking under 1:00 remaining.

Couch took the snap, but then the play was blown dead for replay review. The NFL was using the buzzer system at the time, and though the ball had been snapped the game was stopped anyway. The crowd was already anxious and angry before the replay ruling because, per NFL rules, once the next play begins, the officials can not go back and review the previous play.

But despite replays showing that referee Terry McAulay was two seconds too late to stop the play, it was stopped. The previous play was reviewed, and it was determined that Morgan never had control of the ball. The Jaguars took possession, and enraged fans started launching plastic beer bottles towards McAulay and his referee mates.

They kept launching…and launching. This went on long enough that security officers scrambled to get the officials and the Jaguars off the field. Some Jaguars players gathered at the 50-yard line, making sure it would take an NFL-like arm from a fan to hit them with whatever was being thrown. McAulay at one point ruled that the game was over. Once things settled down, NFL Commissioner Paul Tagliabue overrode McAulay's decision and ordered the game to continue. Not all of the Jaguars' players returned to the field for the final seconds, which consisted of two kneeldowns to seal the win.

It was a surreal scene. For a few minutes, it was a dangerous scene. It became a bizarre and deflating loss for a Browns team that was 6–6 and still a fringe playoff contender coming into the game. After that game, team owner Al Lerner and president Carmen Policy met with the media—and they probably should not have. They were angry with the officials and under the influence of extreme disappointment, if not more.

"Those bottles are plastic," Policy said when asked about the fans' behavior. "They don't pack much of a wallop."

The Browns went on to finish 7–9. The bottle-throwing became a memorable moment, and it led to the end of plastic bottle sales in the new stadium.

98 Training Camps

Jim Brown ran at Hiram College in rural Portage County. Paul Brown coached there, overseeing grueling practices that molded NFL championship teams. Fans navigated winding roads and crammed into Hiram's campus to see the Browns up close in training camp from 1952 to 1974.

Camp used to be, well, camp. Players stayed in dorms and ate in cafeterias. Fans could get closer to the action—and to their favorite players—than they could at almost any other time. Before the onset of formal offseason training programs and year-round training, training camps were for conditioning and team bonding as much as they were for offensive installation and eventual roster decisions.

In today's NFL, veteran players report for camp 15 days before the first preseason game. A mandatory off day is written into each team's camp schedule after five consecutive days of work. Most teams formally close camp around the third preseason game. Since the 1990s, the Browns have held camp at their usual day-to-day headquarters in Berea.

For the first six years of their existence, the Browns held training camp at Bowling Green State University in Northwest Ohio. After their long camp run at Hiram, they held camp at Kent State University from 1975 to 1981 before moving north to Lakeland Community College in Kirtland, about 20 miles east of Cleveland, from 1982 to 1991.

Those mid- to late-1980s Browns were rock stars, and their camp practices were wild and well attended. Camp crowds at Lakeland have reached urban-legend status. Thousands of fans lined the practice fields, often causing traffic jams at the Route 306 exits of Interstate 90. Players stayed in dorms on site, and fans would swarm for autographs and pictures between practice sessions.

In the Haslam era, the Browns explored moving training camp to the University of Akron and to Columbus. The team announced it would be accepting bids and drew interest on some level from both Bowling Green and Hiram. Discussions with Ohio Dominican University in Columbus heated up to the point that some school officials believed they'd be hosting the Browns before those talks fell apart. The Browns had a long list of demands, and Ohio Dominican would have needed to make some major fixes and additions to be able to host the Browns for three or four weeks each summer.

The new NFL collective bargaining agreement established in 2011 basically eliminated two-a-day practices and shortened the length of training camps. Between that and the amount of money teams spend on weight rooms, locker rooms, and treatment centers at their own facilities, more teams are holding training camps at their year-round practice facilities. Some teams don't have the room to open camp practices to the public. The Browns don't have an ideal setup; they can host up to 5,000 fans for camp practices in Berea. In recent years the Browns have instituted an online ticketing policy so fans can reserve spots for training camp practices, which remain free.

The Browns' building, originally constructed in 1991, has been remodeled and expanded several times during the team's new era. During camp, players stay in a local hotel and fans park at nearby Baldwin-Wallace University, where the Browns conducted their day-to-day operations before moving to the new facility.

99 Jim Donovan and Doug Dieken

Doug Dieken has missed two Browns games since the early 1970s. A longtime standout at left tackle, Dieken is the color analyst on the team's radio broadcasts.

Jim Donovan has been the team's play-by-play man since 1999. Donovan previously called NFL games on national television in addition to multiple Olympics and other high-profile events. Partly for professional purposes and partly because he's an obsessive sports fan, Donovan often listens to things like tennis and international soccer on the radio as he tries to perfect his craft and listens to how other radio broadcasters describe the action.

His "Run, William, Run" call from the Browns' 2002 season finale has become a part of new-Browns lore, but that's partly because William Green's 64-yard touchdown run helped push the Browns to what was their only playoff appearance in their first 20 years back in the NFL.

Donovan is the longtime sports director at WKYC Channel 3 in Cleveland. He and Dieken also do local Browns shows and other team-related programming, and in a football-crazed place like Cleveland they're as popular and as recognizable as many of the team's current and recent players.

"It's just two guys sitting around talking football like we have tickets to the game," Donovan said. "I can be very emotional. Doug takes the emotion out of it. It's been a pleasure to work with him for all these years."

Donovan has been known to study rosters and depth charts at all hours of the night, obsessing over things like where the Chargers' backup fullback played in college and proper pronunciations of players who might make a special teams tackle. Dieken is still often around the team, too, collecting the kinds of insights that current players are willing to share with former players—and not necessarily when other cameras and microphones are around.

"I'm just there to laugh or fill in the blanks," Dieken said. "The play-by-play guy does all the work. I've been fortunate to work with some great guys and Jimmy is one of them. He's an immense talent, and he's a fanatic about it."

Donovan missed the 2011 season while recovering from a bone marrow transplant. Diagnosed with leukemia in 2000 when he was 43, Donovan took chemotherapy treatments and rarely talked about his sickness. While recovering from the bone marrow transplant, Donovan had a bad reaction to some medication, causing his fever to spike to 105 degrees for five days. It was so bad that he believed he was going to die and became delirious.

When he speaks about it now, he jokes that he was so delirious that he believed "that the Browns made the Super Bowl." But he was back in the radio booth that September, and the Browns did not make the Super Bowl.

Per mandate from his doctor, Dieken stayed home from the Browns' 2017 trip to London due to what we now know was a minor illness. That was the first game he missed since 1989. He didn't miss many before then, either. Dieken joined the Browns' radio team in 1985, a year after he retired after 14 years as an offensive tackle. Dieken made 194 consecutive starts from 1971 to 1984 and ranks fourth in team history with 203 games played. For perspective, that's 36 more games than Joe Thomas played.

After that London trip, Dieken was back in the booth and back to being his usual sarcastic self by the next game.

Donovan has many times rolled his eyes at the Browns, but on the air he's always projected energy and generally has projected positivity. Dieken, who turned 70 in early 2019, has said he has no real plans to retire. If the Browns ever start winning, he'd love to be along for the ride. And he's certainly seen enough of the alternative to have earned that chance.

100 The Mangini Cruiser

Eric Mangini's annual football camp in his hometown of Hartford, Connecticut, provides an opportunity for kids to rub elbows with NFL coaches and players. The camp has often provided scholarships to attendees to later attend college exposure camps.

In 2009, the camp that's done a bunch of good work was in the news with a negative spin. Headed into his first season as Browns coach, Mangini chartered a bus and brought all 19 Browns rookies to the camp to serve as volunteers.

By the NFL's collective bargaining agreement, the trip had to be voluntary. But it wasn't, especially given that Mangini was serving as head coach and director of all things football. Especially for undrafted rookies or late-round picks, blowing off the camp wasn't an option. They loaded a bus Friday morning for a trip that lasted more than 10 hours.

At least some of the players weren't happy. Their agents were angry, too, and went to the media. At an otherwise slow time for NFL news, all of a sudden the Browns and their power-hungry coach were making headlines for a bus trip, of all things. And a football camp for kids.

Mike Florio, founder of the popular ProFootballTalk.com website, dubbed the bus "The Mangini Cruiser." In one of his posts on the trip, Florio wrote that the trip was "all part of the reality in Cleveland that Mangini rules the roost with an iron fist. As one source explained it, even GM George Kokinis is 'scared to death' of the guy."

That turned out to be pretty accurate. Kokinis only lasted in the job until early November.

Florio later confirmed that the NFL Players Association investigated the trip for violations of the collective bargaining agreement regarding mandatory activities and time spent at the team facility.

Because of the public backlash, Mangini rode the bus back to Cleveland with the 19 rookies and four staffers after the Saturday camp. The rookies were dropped off at the team hotel around 3:00 AM, and Mangini and the staffers then unloaded the equipment the Browns had taken to the camp. In all, the bus trip from Cleveland to Hartford and back covered 20 hours and 20 minutes.

At the beginning of the ride back to Cleveland, an undrafted rookie defensive back named Bryan Williams pretended as if he was a flight attendant making an announcement to a plane full of passengers.

"We'd like to welcome Eric Mangini," Williams said.

Some on the bus laughed. Mangini didn't. Williams got cut a few weeks later. There's no telling whether his joke had anything to do with that.